HOW ROBOTS INFLUENCE FUTURE

US MARKET DEVELOPMENT

JOHN LOK

Copyright © John Lok
All Rights Reserved.

Contents

Preface

Advances in artificial intelligence (AI) technology is for the progress in critical areas, such as health, education, energy, economy inclusion, social welfare and the environment. Whether AI can bring positive or negative impaction to influence human job nature change. How AI influences future US market development?

Thus, it brings this question: Whether (AI) robotic workers can be instead of traditional human workers in these different new markets to bring positive or negative impaction to change human job nature change? In recent years, machines had been used to be human's tasks in the performance of certain tasks related to intelligence , such as aspects of image recognition. Experts also forecast that rapid progress in the field of specialized artificial intelligence will continue. Then, it also brings this question: Does (AI) exceed that of human performance on more and more tasks to replace human jobs? If it is truth, will some of human jobs to be disappeared? (AI) will be instead of human some simple jobs, then unemployment rate to the low skillful and low educated workers will be increased. What od US market will be improved to develop by AI rapidly ?

This book divides two parts. Part one explains how (AI) brings negative impaction to influence low skill labor unemployment number raises , due to human job will disappear. Part one explains how (AI) brings positive impaction to influence productivity and efficiency raising , even assisting any country itself economic growth.

In chapter one, I shall explain what the (AI) functions are benefited to human and I shall indicate whether how it can impact human job nature as well as I shall explain whether (AI) can influence to change to human job market to be better or worse in future global labor market to bring negative impaction.

In chapter two, I shall indicate how (AI) will influence global economic technology productivity change as well as I shall indicate whether (AI) technology can impact global service management industry development to bring positive impaction.

In chapter three, I shall indicate whether (AI) technology will influence digital industry economic change as well as I shall indicate whether (AI) technology can influence developing countries' economic change and health and manufacturing change , even global economic change in our future life to bring positive impaction.

This book is suitable to any students who expect to make personal judgement and analysis to concern whether how (AI) technology will impact our life and it can influence global economic and job market change in our future.

If one factory or one office only applies artificial intelligent robotic machine men to replace human labors to help its different departments to do any tasks, whether can its (AI) robotic machine men help them to raise productive efficiencies ? If one restaurant or one shopping center only apply (AI) robotic machine men to help to serve clients, whether can its (AI) robotic machine men help them to improve service performance? Is it better to apply half manual labors and half (AI) robotic machine men to work in one organization in order to raise productive efficiencies or improve service performance?

In my this book, I shall indicate some cases to explain how and why (AI) robotic machine men can either raise productive efficiencies or improve service performance or they can't either raise productive efficiencies or improve service performance in any situations. Managers or employees can evaluate whether how to apply (AI) robotic machine men to assist them to work in their workplaces in order to achieve the most beneficial advantages to their organization's different departments' raising productivity and efficiency and service performance improvement aims.

This book concerns how to apply artificial intelligence technology to apply to US some consumption market. I shall explain how to apply (AI) technology to these America consumption market to raise their food or product productivity growth efficiently. I shall indicate some popular American consumption market of some consumer products and foods as well as manufacturers' production of material consumption products. This book brings two questions:

(1) Can apply (AI) technology to raise these US food and product productivity growth?

(2) Will these US food and product quality influence to be poor after (AI) technology is applied to raise productivity growth ?

The USfuture manufacturers material and consumers products will be influenced by robotic technology : How to apply (AI) technology to raise future U.S. tobacco productivity growth? How to apply (AI) technology to raise steel material productivity growth for manufacturing industries? How to apply (AI) technology to raise minerals productivity growth for U.S. manufacturing industries? How to apply (AI) technology to improve orange fruit and vegetables logistic transportation speed in efficient way in warehouses? How to apply (AI) technology to improve U.S. alcohol logistic transportation speed in efficient way in warehouse? How to apply (AI) technology to improve U.S. energy service performance to satisfy energy users' needs? How to apply (AI) technology to improve wine and tea logistic transportation speed in warehouse? How to apply (AI) technology to improve pork logistic transportation speed in warehouse? How to apply (AI) technology to improve U.S. tourism entertainment service performance to satisfy traveler needs? How to apply (AI) technology to improve sugar logistic transportation speed in warehouse? How to apply (AI) technology to raise lighting product productivity growth ?

Prologue

Can (AI) impact human job nature?

How can (AI) influence labor market?
How can human society job nature
to be changed to
artificial intelligent society?
Why does human need artificial intelligence machines?

How does artificial intelligence
influence future working changing
in automation employment and

productivity aspects?

Is artificial intelligence possible
to replace labor ?
Can (AI) technology replace human
labour nature of work?
Why can artificial intelligence satisfy
human needs?
     Is artificial intelligence one good choice
for human future technological benefit?
     What is relationship between
(AI) and economy growth? p.46-60
How can artificial intelligence technology influence economy?
Can (AI) influence us economy
growth?
How can artificial intelligence
impact global economy growth?
How can (AI) influence GDP of high income
countries in the next ten years?
How can artificial intelligence
impact on workplace?
What is the relationship
between (AI) and (CRM)?
Can (AI) technology
impact on customer relationship
management (CRM) ?

What is relationship between
(AI) and digital economy? P.61-81

How can (AI) technology influence digital
economy?

What is the relationship between
(AI) and global digital economy development?
     Could work activities in China be
automated making in the nation with the world's largest automation

potential?

How does (AI) technology influence the future of employment change?

How can artificial intelligence impact global economy growth?

Why will (AI) technology grow economic development ?

How can (AI) technology impact to global economic and social and psychological changes?

Will (AI) technology influence digital economy change to manufacturing industry ?

What is artificial intelligence potential benefits and ethical considerations?

How can (AI) technology influence to global health care economy development?

Reference

Chapter 2

Can Artificial intelligence apply to digital-Transformation on jobs to raise productivity

1.1 Apply (AI) technology to raise p.82-95 U.S. steel, aluminum, cooper mineral productivity growth

Chapter 3

Can robots raise productive efficiency to raise logistic transportation speed

2.1 Apply (AI) technology to improve fruit and vegetable soft drink logistic transportation speed in efficient way p.96-120 in warehouse

2.2 Applying (AI) technology to improve global daily food logistic transpotation

CHAPTER I

Future US artificial intelligent marketing development

(AI) -driven automation
industry development

1.1 (AI) - driven automation industry development how to influence work nature change to bring negative impaction

(AI) -driven automation industry will create wealth and expand economy growth to any countries, but it will be accompanied by changed in the skills that workers need to learn. One of main ways that technology increases productivity is by decreasing the number of labor hours needed to create a unit of output. It implies (AI) technology will influence low educated and low skillful labor number to be decreased (reduction employment number).

Although, AI automation can raise efficiency and productivity, but due to manufacturer concentrate on bring (AI) robotic automation skills to manufacture any products, it will lead future many human jobs disappeared, finally, it will bring negative impact to bring many low skillful labours will lose their jobs , due to robots can replace them to do different kinds of jobs. (AI) -driven automation industry will create wealth and expand economy growth to any countries, but it will be accompanied by changed in the skills that workers need to learn. One of main ways that technology increases productivity is by decreasing the number of labor hours needed to create a unit of output. It implies (AI) technology will influence low educated and low skillful labor number to be decreased (reduction employment number).

In contrast, technological change tended to work in a different direction throughout the nowadays. The advance of computer and the internet raised the relative productivity of higher skilled workers. So, routine-intensive occupations that focused on predictable tasks disappearance, such as switch board, operators, filming checkers, travel agents and assembling line workers etc. were particularly replaced by new technologies. All these human jobs will be replaced from AI automation technology after ten years in possible.

In positively view point, (AI) driven-automation will make many workers more productive and increase demand for certain skills. Consequently, new jobs are likely to be directly create in areas , such as the development and supervision of (AI) as well as indirectly created in a range of areas throughout the economy as higher incomes lead to expanded demand. So, it is only the high skilled labors who can learn how to supervise or manage or control (AI) robots how to work in order to raise productive efficiency , whose skills will increase need. Due to their skills shortage, so they will be difficult to be replaced from (AI). It means that this high skillful (AI) supervision labours won't lose jobs in the future. Otherwise, they will raise wage, due to skill shortage in the (AI) industry job market future.

However, today, it may be challenging to predict exactly which jobs will be most immediately affected by (AI) driven-automation. The reason is because (AI) is not a single technology, but rather a collection of technologies that are felt unevenly through the economy to influence job changing both negatively and positively. In positively view point, (AI) driven-automation will make many workers more productive and increase demand for certain skills. Consequently, new jobs are likely to be directly create in areas , such as the development and supervision of (AI) as well as indirectly created in a range of areas throughout the economy as higher incomes lead to expanded demand. Otherwise, in negatively view point, many traditional human needed (demand) skillful jobs will be threatened by automation are highly concentrated among lower-paid, lower-skilled and less -educated workers. It means automation will cause pressure on demand for this group, pressure and employment, if (AI) can replace the low skilled and less educated workers' jobs. Thus, (AI) will have negative influence to impact on the labor market.

(AI) capabilities will enable automation of some tasks that have long required human labor. Why can (AI) replace some simple human jobs? For example, advances in robotics are expanding machines' abilities to interact with and sharp the physical world. Combined , (AI) and robotics will give rise to smarter machines that can perform more sophisticated functions than ever before and brings more advantages that humans have exercised. This will permit automation of many tasks now performed by human workers and could change the shape of the labor market and human activity.

1.2 How (AI) influences labor market

Today, it may be challenging to predict exactly which jobs will be most immediately affected by (AI)-driven automation. Because (AI) is not a single technology, but rather a collection of technologies that are applied to specific tasks.

Some specific predictions are possible based on the current (AI) technology. For example, driving jobs and house cleaning jobs, bank counter service jobs, telephone enquiry service operators. Restaurant cooking jobs, simple accounting record service jobs etc. that require relatively less education to perform. Advancements in computer vision and related technologies have made the feasibility of fully appear more likely, potentially displacing some workers in driving-dominant professions. Seemingly similar robot, for which the operational tasks is less specific of navigating to a specific destination when following a set of given rules and preserving safety.

In the future, the effects of (AI) on the labor market in the decade ahead will continue the trend toward skill-biased change that computerization and communication innovations have driven in recent decades. Thus, some human driving occupation will be disappeared or replaced by (AI) automation driven. For example, bus drivers, light truck or delivery services drivers, heavy and tractor-trailer truck drivers, school drivers, tax drivers, travel bus drivers.

However, (AI) technology could enable some workers to focus time on other job responsibilities, boosting their productivity, and actually raised wage growth among those still holding the reshaped jobs. For example, salespeople, who currently spend a considerable amount of time driving could find themselves able to do other work when a car drives them from place to place, or inspectors and appraisers could fill out paperwork, when their car drives itself. This (AI) -driven technology should make these workers more productive, with (AI) -driven technology serving as a complement, not a substitute. New jobs will also likely be created, both in existing occupations cheaper transportation costs with lower prices and increase demand for products and all the related occupations, such as service and fulfillment, and in new occupations not currently foreseeable.

What kind of jobs will be created by (AI) technology? Predicting future job growth is extremely difficult, due to it depends on technologies or substitute for existing today as well as they may complement or substitute for existing human skills and jobs. However, (AI) will also lead to substantial indirect job creation to the degree it raises productivity and wages, it may also lead to higher consumption that would support additional jobs from high-end draft production to restaurant and retail. The future(AI)

" augmented intelligence", the technology's role is as assisting and expanding the productivity of individuals rather than replacing human work. Thus, based on the biased-technical change framework, demand for labor will likely increase the most in the areas where humans complement (AI) automation technologies. For example, (AI) technology , such as IBM's Watson may improve early detection of some cancers or other illnesses, but a human healthcare professional is needed to work with patients to understand and translate patients' symptoms, inform patients of treatment options, and guide patients through treatment plans. Shipping companies may also partner workers who pick up and deliver products over the last feet with (AI) enabled autonomous vehicles that move workers efficiently from site to site. In such cases, (AI) augments what a human is able to do and allows individuals to either be move effective in their specially task or to operate on a larger scale. Thus, it seems (AI) technology will also create new jobs, raise productivities and workers' efficiencies.

1.3 Redefining management in
the workforce of artificial intelligence

● Change management

In the future, due to artificial intelligence influences to some kind of human jobs nature. So, the kind of human jobs of management methods will also need to change to adapt the artificial intelligence technology input to their organizations. It will cause challenges for every executive and manager if who won't have effort to manage their teams how to apply artificial intelligence technology to work efficiently and easily. For example, division of labor will change among humans and machines will increase. Thus, companies will have to adapt their training performance and talent strategies how to emphasize on work that how to make human judgment and skills and experimentation. Thus, (IA)'s greatest impact will be on administrative coordination and control tasks, such as scheduling , resource allocation.

In fact, mangers will encounter this challenges: How to apply human experience and expertise to judge critical business decisions and practices when the information available is insufficient to suggest a successful course of action? Due to this kind of work will require new skills and mindsets. I shall indicate these change management methods to adapt (AI) technology. Such as: administration and routine tasks, scheduling , allocation of resources and reporting will fall within the intelligence machines, responsibilities that have long been reserved for humans. For example, a typical store manager or a lead nurse at a nursing home most constantly arrange shift schedules, accounting for staff members' absences owing to illness, vacation time or sudden departures.

Thus, the managers need to learn how to arrange new division of labor within the organizations after (AI) technology had been implemented to the organization. Artificial intelligence is currently influencing into once considered exclusive to humans: assessing and acting on human emotions and personality traits. The influences to managers need to change their strategies to adapt (AI) technology implements include such as below:

Firstly, managers need to spend the bulk of their time on coordination and control tasks from intelligent system implements. Their time spending on these major three aspects from impact of intelligent system: coordinate and control, solve problems and collaborate and people and community , strategy and innovation three aspects. Thus (AI) will influence managers need to change their judgment method to teach whose teams how to adapt the (AI) system operations in any organizations.

Secondly, (AI) will influence top, middle and low level management needs to change to adapt the (AI) technology operations to any owned (AI) technology organizations in the future. Intelligent machines must be trained in context. Just like humans , on-the-job training is a requirement for such machines because they typically arrive with only very general capabilities. To get the most from (AI), managers at all levels must participate in the instructional experience and in the learning process and provides managers' familiarity with such systems on these aspects, e.g. How the system works and generate advice, how the system has a proven track record , how the system provides convincing explanations , how the system can make simple rule- based decisions.

Thirdly, managers need to learn how to make judgment more accurate (AI) systems assistance. Although (AI) will invariably take on more routine work and even augment human decision-making, it won't judgment work, the application of human experience and expertise to critical business decisions when the information available is insufficient to suggest a successful course of action or reliable enough to suggest an obvious course of action. For a sense of the nature of judgment work, consider big data marketing and sales analytics. Such analytics often provide insights that can inform promotional campaigns, including predicting which promotions will generate desired sales brand further into the future, marketing executives need use judgment, combining analytics with their own and others' insight and experience.

The application of experience and expertise to critical business decisions and practice represents the real value of human judgment. But, when artificial intelligent machines are implemented to any organizations to assist the low, middle and top level management to make any business judgment. These forms of judgment work that managers can gather data interpretation, idea development more absolute from (AI) machine assistance. Thus, why these level management executives need to learn how to apply (AI) machines to help them to make any business judgment more accurate.

● How (AI) influences organizational change

Consequently creative and social intelligence will be in even greater demand as (AI) makes in management and the workforce. This development will represent a long term trend in labor markets , one characterized by intensifying demand and reward for social skills with a growing desire for creative capabilities, managers will seek to fashion of ideas and hypotheses from inside and outside of the enterprise to shape solutions to their most pressing business problems. Thus, (AI) will influence overall organizational team members who have chance to participate any decision to make more accurate business judgment.

Many managers mistakenly view judgment work as only an individual discipline, failing to appreciate that it can also involve decide interpersonal and organizational practices. In more complex settings, judgment is typically a collective outcome of individuals' and teams' diverse perspectives, insights and experiences. And often , the resulting choices are better informed than decisions that an individual would have arrived at on his or her own.

Thus, when any organizations apply (AI) technology to assist managers to gather data and ideas to make any judgment. In these cases, organizations can create the conditions for effective collective judgment by establishing structures , such as " shadow advisory boards" that prompt managers and employees to source and synthesize multiple perspectives. Thus, a traditional organization (firm) might freshen its thinking is t put together a shadow advisory board, comprised of young, digital people who can apply (AI) machine assistance to make judgment work more accurate whether related to people development, problem-solving or strategizing and innovating for considerable degrees of creative and social intelligence.

Thus, on the one hand, (AI) technology machine augmentation and automation can give these advantages to human (organization managers) , e.g. developing people and community, solving problems and collaborating, coordinating and controlling work, shaping strategy and leading innovation. Besides, on the other hand, the next generation managers need have these individual attitude to treat intelligent machines to be as colleagues.

When, judgment is a human skill, intelligent machines can accelerate human learning that supports it, assisting in data -driven simulations, scenarios and search and discovery activities. Focuses on judgment work, some decisions require insight beyond what data can tell them. This is the sweet sport for human judgment, the application of experience and expertise to critical business decisions and practices. Thus, managers will also need to find ways to learn how to use digital (AI) technologies to tap into the knowledge and judgment of partners, customer external stakeholders and role models in other industries after the (AI) machine had been implemented to the organization.

Future works change:
Automation, employment
and productivity

2.1 How (AI) influences employment

Human future " micro to macro" industry trends will be affected business strategy and public policy by (AI) technology. In the future (AI) technology will influence those six themes: productivity and growth, natural resources, labor markets, the evolution of global financial markets, the economic impact of technology and innovation and urbanization. However, (AI) technology will bring economic benefits of tackling gender inequality, a new global competition, Chinese innovation and digital globalization.

Nowadays, advances in robotics artificial intelligence, and machine learning are in a new age of automation, as machines match or outperform human performance in a development to any countries. For example, automation of activities can enable businesses to improve performance by reducing errors and improving quality and speed, and in some cases achieving outcomes that go beyond human capabilities. For example, some research indicated automation could raise productivity growth globally by 0.8 to 1.4 % annually; more than 2,000 work activities across 800 occupations. When less than 5% of all occupations can be automated using demonstrated technologies about 60% of all occupations have at least 30% of constituent activities that could be automated. Many occupations will change that will be automated away: Activities most susceptible to automation involve physical activities, in highly structured and predictable environments, as well as the collection and processing of data. They are most prevalent in manufacturing , accommodation and food service and retail trade and include some middle-skill jobs. For example, such as natural language processing is a key factor. Beyond technical feasibility, the cost of technology competition with labor including skills and supply and demand dynamics, performance benefits including and beyond labor cost savings, and social and regulatory acceptance will be affected by (AI) automation technology. Thus, (AI) automation will impact to influence global employment in those aspects as below:

Firstly, assuming that people are displaced by automation will find other employment. The anticipated shift in the activities in the labor force is of a similar order as the long-term shift away from agriculture and decreases in manufacturing share of employment. Both of manufacturing and agriculture industries which would be accompanied by the creation of new types of work not foreseen at the time.

Secondly, for business, the performance benefits of automation are relatively clear. Thus, the businessmen have opportunities for their micro economies to benefits from the productivity growth potential and macro economies to benefit to encourage continued progress and innovation , investment and market incentives. At the same time, employers must innovate policies to help workers and institutions adapt to the impact on employment.

This will likely include rethinking education and training, income support and safety nets , as well as support for those dislocated, when employees need to leave themselves homes to move to other cities to learn new (AI) automation works. Thus, individuals in the workplace will need to engage move comprehensively with machines as part of their everyday activities, and acquire new skills that will be in demand in the new automation age. Consequently , the scale of shifts in the labor force over many decades that automation technologies can be a similar order to the long -term technology -enables shifts in the developed countries' workforces away from agriculture in the 21 th century. Those shifts did not result in long-term mass unemployment because they were accompanied by the creation of new types of work not foreseen at the time. However, human will still be needed in the workforce when the total productivity gains are caused by (AI) technology.

2.2 What occupations will be influenced by (AI) technology.

In the future, scientists predict that these occupations will be influenced by (AI) technology mostly. They include : retail salespeople, food and beverage service workers, language or translation teachers, health practitioners. Since these work activities have a more relevant occupations are made up of a range of activities with different potential for (AI) automation . For example, a retail salesperson will spend more time interacting with customers, stocking shelves , or ringing up sales. Each of these activities is distinct and requires different capabilities to perform successfully.

Thus, these job activities have similar simple control characteristics. Simple activities include greet customers, answer questions about products and services, clean and maintain work areas, demonstrate product feature process sales and transactions. All these activities can have similar simple activities in order to (AI) machines can be learn how to do these activities from (AI) technology . For example, the capability perception includes sensory perception, cognitive capabilities, such as retrieving automation, recognizing known patterns(supervised learning), logical reasoning problem solving.

Thus, (AI) machine is such human, which has feeling and emotion, such as social and emotional sensing, judgement reasoning methods, natural language understanding and physical capabilities, such as mobility , navigation, gross motor skill, fine motor skills. It seems that the future, (AI) human invents machines which will have these human characteristics to do human similar behavioral job duties more easily and efficiently. It implies these above human occupations will be replaced by (AI) human invention machines in the future. Due to (AI) creation, it is possible to cause unemployment number of these above workers will increase because (AI) machines can do their similar job behavioral activities.

Consequently, employers won't need to employ many of these skillful labor. Otherwise, they can buy less number (AI) machines to attempt to do whose job activities more easily and efficiently. So, it seems (AI) machines will have more high work performance to replace these occupation workers' work performance. Finally, these occupation worker unemployment number will only increase when the (AI) machines had been invented to achieve to do their work behavioral activities absolutely success in the future.

2.3 Whether (A) technology machine labor
will replace human worker more or assist
human worker more

There is no single agreed definition of a robot how outcome of a task that is completed without human intervention. When some definitions require the task to be completed by a physical machine moves and respond to its environment, other definitions use the term robot in connection with tasks completed by software , without physical embodiment.

However, to answer the question : Whether (AI) technology machine labor will replace human worker more or assist human worker more. I shall indicate some examples to let readers to judge whether (AI) technology can create new jobs or reduce old jobs.

Firstly, I shall explain what (AI) function is. (AI) is a service robot that performs useful tasks for humans or equipment excluding industrial automation application . Thus, the classification of a robot into industrial robot or service robot is done according to its intended application. It is also a personal service robot or a service robot for personal used for a non commercial task, usually by lay persons . Examples are domestic servant robot, and pet exercising robot. It is also a professional service robot or a service robot for professional used for a commercial task, usually operated by a properly trained operator. Examples, are cleaning robot for public places, delivery robot in offices or hospitals, fire-fighting robot, rehabilitation robot and surgery robot in hospitals. Thus, these functions will be future (AI) application to our daily life necessaries or business necessaries.

However, some authors agree (AI) will bring negative outcomes of automation, due to raise competiveness, reduce human job nature. Otherwise, other authors argue (AI) will bring positive outcomes of automation, due to raise productivities, job creation, assist humans work.

On the positive outcome hand, robots can increase productivity . This is particularly important for small-to medium sized businesses both are in developed and developing countries economies. It also enables large companies to increase their competitiveness through faster product development and delivery. Increased use of robot is also enabling companies in high cost countries to re shore, or bring back to their domestic base parts of the supply chain that will have previously outsourced to sources of cheaper labor. Currently , the greater threat to employment is not a automation, but an inability to remain competitive. Automation has led overall to an increase in labor demand and positive impact on wages. The reason is that the middle-income/middle-skilled jobs have reduced as a proportion of overall contribution to employment and earnings leading to fears of increasing income inequality, the skills range within the middle income bracket is large. Thus, robots are driving an increase in demand for workers at the higher -skilled and with a positive impact on wages. This issue is how to enable middle-income earners in the lower-income range to unskilled or retain. Finally, the (AI) positive impact supporter who argue the future will be robots and humans can work together.

However, on the negative outcome hand, robots can substitute labor activities, but don't replace jobs. They believe that less than 10% of jobs are fully automatable. Increasingly , robots are used to complement and augment labor activities, the net impact on jobs and the quality of work is positive. Automation can provide the opportunity for humans to focus on higher-skilled, higher-quality and higher-paid tasks. Robots can improve productivity when they are applied to tasks that which perform more efficiently and to a higher and more consistent level of quality than humans. For example, increased productivity is enabling some firms, such as Whirlpool, Caterpillar and Ford Motors company in the US restructure their supply chains, bringing back parts of the manufacturing process to the country of origin. Thus, productivity gains due to robotics and automation are important not just at the company level, but also for build industry and nation competitiveness.

I suppose that productivity can be raised. What are the impacts of robots on employment? Firstly, the main focus of development has been on personal entertainment, which does not drive worker productivity (manufacturing production). When the internet (information and communication technology (ICT)) innovation. This is borne and by findings that manufacturing productivity, which has been driven by innovations in automation rather than consumer technologies, has government strongly than productivity in the services sectors of the economy in most nature economies. It seems (AI) automation will create many jobs in internet communication entertainment game industry. For example, many young people like to use internet to play any electronic games from computer or mobile at home or outside home conveniently. Thus, (AI) automation will increase demand to be invented to any new entertainment game from internet channel. It will need to employ many (AI) entertainment game inventors to create many automation entertainment games. Thus, (AI) automation in internet entertainment game industry will need human (AI) entertainment game inventors to invent the knowledge-based capital of (AI) automation entertainment games. The (AI) entertainment game inventors will need own research and development skills, form specific skills, organizational know-how skills, databased knowledge, design and various forms of intellectual property to do these (AI) automation entertainment game invention occupations in the future.

International Federation Of Robotics(2016) indicated that China will be as a major robotics manufacturer and user of robots, benefiting from jobs created by robot manufacturing and productivity gains from robot use. Chins had sold of robots to any one single market every year since 2017 year. The Chinese government has included a focus on robotics in its 10 year strategy. In order to achieve its target of a robot density of 150 units per 10, 000 workers by 2020 year. Thus, Chinese companies will have to install around 650,000 new industrial robots between 2016 to 2020 year, 2.5 times more than installed globally in 2015 year.

Hence, China (AI) manufacturing industry will need to employ many workers . It implies (AI) manufacturing industry will create many new occupations in China. Also, ministry of economy, trade and industry (2015) also showed that Japan currently has the largest stock of industrial robots in operations, primarily in the automation industry. Driven by a rapidly aging population and low productivity rates, the Japanese government has sights on a 20-fold increase in the use of robots in the non-manufacturing sector and a three-fold growth rate of labor productivity in the service sector both by 2020 year. Thus, it also implies Japan will need many robots to be provide to service industry. Due to robots will provide to serve any businessmen's clients. Thus, it is possible that the service workers won't be dismissed as well as it is depended on the serving job nature to decide whether Japan's service workers can still serve to their employer when the service (AI) robots are applied to whose employers.

Consequently, it seems that (AI) can create employment, Ministry of economy, trade and industry (2015) showed that such as China will develop the major (AI) automation manufacturing industry. The (AI) employers will need to employ many workers to manufacture any these different kinds of (AI) robots to satisfy China or overseas individual or business buyers needs. But, (AI) can also cause unemployment to the low skillful service workers. Such as if Japan some service businesses choose to buy any (AI) service robots to replace their service staffs to serve their clients. It is possible that the service staffs will be dismissed, due to (AI) robots can do such as their same service job duties to achieve better service performance. Thus, today, it is increasingly common for people to use robots in various situations at home and in retail stores, hotels and hospitals these service industries. Robots are classified into server types based on their functionality (service and utility robots or those designed to communicate with humans) and appearance (humanoid robots or mechanical robots). The type of robot, to which each country allocated particular importance in the advance of robotics, reflects the sense of values and preferences of its population. Thus, if the country has high population needs to use robots, then they will influence either more new jobs creation or more old job loss in the country's (AI) manufacturing or (AI) service industries both. For example, Japan respondents often associate the term " robot " with humanoid robots that can communicate with human and they have a high level of familiarity with robot. The US has the highest level of robot utilization at home and in retail stores with its people being the most enthusiastic about the future use of robots. Germany shows a strong tendency to consider robots for industrial purposes and its people feel strong effort to the presence of robots in their households.

In conclusion, to judge whether how (AI) will influence the country's employment to be better or worse. It will depend on the country home buyers (users) or business buyers (users) how to use (AI) for their daily needs. If the country , such as US retail stores need to use (AI) , it will have possible to reduce some or many retail service workers. Even, if the country , such as Japan has many home users need to use (AI) , it will not influence the employment market. Otherwise, it will raise (AI) salespeople numbers. Even, if the country, such as Germany and China will have many (AI) manufacturers, then it will create many (AI) manufacturing occupations for these (AI) manufactory workers.

Consequently, (AI) robots manufacturing and service needs will have positive or negative impact to any country's employment. It will depend on the (AI) service provision and service workers' job nature as well as the manufacturing workers of (AI) knowledge level to decide their employment chance in their country's employment market.

What does artificial intelligence(AI) mean?
- What (AI) function is?

Some scientists explain that artificial intelligence means which is an expert system, computer software that embodies a portion of the specialized knowledge of a human portion in a specific, narrow domain, owns decision making ability of human expert. The (AI)technology is based on the premise that what makes a person an expert is years of experience that enables who recognizes certain patterns in a problem as being similar to pattern. For example, in the future artificial intelligence system can be applied to control air traffic, design to computer configuration, medical diagnosis, instruction/training, speech/interpretation, monitoring to (nuclear plant), planning to mission, factory scheduling, prediction weather, repairing telephone, automatic driving etc. different industries.

Artificial intelligence characteristics include: creative, adaptive , common sense, fact processing, quick replication, broad focus permanent and consistent skill. Otherwise, traditional computer expert system disadvantage includes perishable, unpredictable, slow reproduction, expensive, slow reproduction, slow processing lacks inspiration, needs instruction, narrow focus only machine knowledge. So, artificial intelligence is a branch of computer science devoted to creating computer to influence software and hardware to attempt to create human intelligence or human intelligent behavior. It is learning from experience, responds flexibility in situation that are, new or not anticipated.

Thus, (AI) can be learnt programmed knowledge to solve problems, using reasoning in solving problem, understanding and inferring facts and rules, recognizing the relative importance of different elements in a situation. In summary, artificial intelligence is concerned with two basic ideas mainly: The first idea, it involves studying the thought processes of humans to understand what intelligence is; the second idea, it deals with representing thought processes using companies to create artificially intelligent entities for testing the theories of intelligence.

- Can (AI) impact human job nature?

Human need concern this question: Will artificial intelligence (AI) reduce some human jobs in order to instead of replacing machines to do? Due to artificial intelligence is the ability of machines to do thing, that people would require intelligence. For example, artificial intelligence machine man driving(self-driver), it (AI) machine man driving research is an attempt to discover and describe aspects of human intelligence that can be simulated by driving machine functions. Alternatively, (AI) mathematical research may be another viewed as an attempt to develop a mathematical theory function to describe the abilities and actions of things (natural or man-made) exhibiting intelligent behavior and server as a design of intelligent calculation machine function.

Why do humans need artificial intelligence machines to instead of traditional human service job? For example, can artificial intelligence machine man (self-driving) driver drive to replace human driver? I shall compare the differences between humans and computers : The characteristics of humans are good at recognizing various things, either seen before or not, recognizing the relationship patterns between things. Human thinking is common sense reasoning, combining all types of sensory input, acting appropriately in novel situations, learning new things and changing behavior patterns, making decisions , even when given incomplete information, working with noisy, incomplete information gathering behaviors . However, characteristics of computers are good at: The tasks humans do naturally are extremely difficult for a computer program as intelligent, which must be able to do the same kind of tack as humans do naturally.

Hence, (AI) is an combination of many different success and technologies: Linguistics - computational and socio, philosophy-logic, philosophy of mind and of language, electronical engineering -image and speech processing, pattern recognition, robotics, machine learning, neural networks, optimization scheduling, management information system and decision making. So, it is possible that (AI) can impact human job nature to instead of human working behavior in the future.

How can (AI) influence labor market?
● How can human society job nature
to be changed to artificial intelligent society?

From the first intelligent perspective reason view point, artificial intelligence is making machines " intelligent" acting as humans expect people to act. Artificial intelligence has ability to distinguish computer responses from human responses, it owns knowledge to solve expert problem. From another research perspective reason view point, artificial intelligence is the study of how to make computers do things which, at the moment, people do better (Rich & Knight, 1991, p.3).

(AI) researchers are native in a variety of domains, e.g. formal tasks (mathematics, games), tasks (perception, robotics, natural language, common sense reasoning), expert tasks (financial analysis, medical diagnostics, engineering, scientific analysis and other areas).

From the second business perspective reason view point, (AI) is a set of many powerful tools, and methodologies for using those tools to solve business problems. From a programming perspective reason view point, (AI) includes the study of symbolic programming problem solving and search .

From the third human technological perspective reason view point, today's computer can do many well-defined tasks, for example, arithmetic operations, are much faster and more accurate than human beings. However, the computers' interaction with their environment is not very sophisticated yet. How can human test whether a computer has reached the general intelligence level of a human being? Can a computer convince a human interrogator that it is a human? But before thinking of such advanced kinds of machines, human will start developing our own extremely simple " intelligent" machines.

So, it is possible that human society job nature will to be changed to artificial intelligent society when (AI) technology is developed to the mature stage in the future.

● Why does human need artificial intelligence machines?
One of major division in (AI) is between humans who think (AI) is the only serious way of finding out how we (human) work and human who want companies to do very smart things, independently of how we (human) work. This is the important distinction between cognitive scientists vs engineers. One of another major division in (AI) is between symbolic (AI), which represents information through symbols and their relationships. Specific Algorithms are used to process these symbols to solve problems or deduce new knowledge and connectionist. So (AI) , which represents information in network. Biological processes underlying learning, task performance and problem solving are imitated from human mind behaviors. Thus, it is possible that artificial intelligence machines can do the better judgicious behavior to compare human.

● How does artificial intelligence influence future working changing in automation employment and productivity aspects?
In the automation changing influence aspect, as companies increasingly use robots on production lines or algorithms to optimize their logistics manage

inventory, any carry out other core business functions. Technological advances are creating a new automation age in which ever-smarter and more flexible machines will be deployed on an ever larger scale in the marketplace. However, researching artificial intelligence with how influences human working nature. We need to answer these questions: How will automation transform the workplace? What will the implications for employment? And what is likely to be its impact both on productivity in the global economy and on employment?

Advances in robotics, artificial intelligence, and machine learning are growing in a new age of automation as machines match or outperform human performance in a range of work activities, including ones requiring cognitive capabilities. What factors are determined the changing in workplace adoption by artificial intelligence innovation? What advantages are automation? Automation of activities can be enabled businesses to improve performance by reducing errors and improving quality and speed, and achieving outcomes that go beyond human capabilities.

Some scientists indicated based on their scenario modeling. They estimated automation could raise producing growth globally by 0.8 to 1.4 percent annually. Almost, the activities people are paid almost $16 trillion in wages to do in global economy have the potential to be automated by adopting currently demonstrated technology. According to their analysis of more than 2,000 work activities across 800 occupations. When less than 5% of all occupations have of least 30% of activities that could be automated. They also indicated that technical economic and social factors will determine automation. Continued technical progress, for example, in areas such as natural language processing is a key factor beyond technical feasibility , the cost of technology, competition with labor including skills, and supply and demand dynamics, performance benefits including and beyond labor cost savings and social and regulatory acceptance will affect (alter) the scope of automation.

Other some scientists also indicate U.S. country for example, the anticipate shift in the activities in labor force of a similar order of magnitude as the long term sight away from agriculture and decreases in manufacturing. Share of employment in the United States both which were achieved. So, those factors can influence why artificial intelligence technology needs. So, it is possible that future agriculture and manufacturing both industries will apply (AI) technology manufacturer-kind of job nature to raise productivity instead of farmers, fruit picking workers, farming transportation labours as well as factory manufacturing workers and supervisors etc. human-kind of job nature.

● Is artificial intelligence possible to replace labor ?

Not just intelligence, but also debating, if machines are capable of having a conscious minds. Artificial intelligence has those characteristics as below:

On functionalism aspect, artificial intelligence inputs mental states, sensory inputs, (beliefs, desires being in pain feeling) and behavioral outputs. Since mental states are identified by a functional role, which are thoughts to be manifested in various systems. Even, perhaps computers which are physical devices with electronic substrate that inform computations on inputs to give outputs similar to brains which are artificial intelligence composed of part any intrinsic relationship to each other. Thus, artificial intelligence activities is not the whole itself, but into parts or on external influence on the parts.

On dualism aspect, artificial intelligence is a set of views about the relationship between mind are matter. On materialism aspect, it builds the only thing that exists is matter, including consciousness.

On biological naturalism aspect, it is similar a human brain than feels pains makes mental situation. So, artificial intelligence is similar biologist which might to be excited to human labor work. Hence, it seems artificial intelligence can change (alter) or replace human labor work of nature in possible in the future.

● Can (AI) technology replace human labour nature of work?

On technological innovation reason view point, the history development of artificial intelligence studying the intelligence is one of most ancient scientific discipline. The history development of artificial intelligence what aims to achieve human use to sense, learn remember and think, logic probability, decision making and calculation develop from mathematics, instead of replacement human labor functions.

Artificial intelligence history development aim is the scientific analysis of skills in connection and practice with the appearance of computers from 1950 year beginning. The artificial intelligence (AI) can deal with the ultimate challenges. How can (either biological or electronic) mind sense, understand and manipulate a world that is much simple and more complex than itself? And what if would human like to construct something with such capabilities?

The general-purpose software of the early period of (AI) were only able to solve simple tasks effectively and failed when which should be used in a wider range or an more difficult tasks. One of the sources of difficulty was that early software had very few or mix knowledge about the problems which handled, and activities successes by simply syntactic manipulation. Moreover, the other difficulty was that many problems that were tried to solve by the (AI) were untreatable.

The early (AI) software whether trying step sequences based on the basic facts about the problem that should be solved, experimented with different combinations till which found a solution. From the end the 1960 year, developing the so-called expert systems were emphasized. These systems had (sue-based) knowledge base about the field which handled. Till to the beginning of the 1970 year, (Prolog) the logical programming language was born, which was built in the computation realization of a version of the resolution calculus. (Prolog) is a remarkably prevalent tool in developing expert systems (on medical, judiciary and other scopes), but natural language parsers were implemented in this language. Then, in 1981 s, the Japanese announced the fifth generation computer system project, a 10 years plan to build an intelligent computer system that use the (Prolog) language as a machine code. Nowadays, (AI) can be applied any industries, such as car manufacturing industry can use (AI) technological machine-men manufacture car, instead of replacing human labors in factory. Even, in the future, using (AI) machine-men drivers can drive any private cars or public transportation tools, instead of replacing human drivers, e.g. bus, train, tram, ferry etc. Also in the future, machine-men can replace housewives to serve families to do housekeeping clean job , e.g. cleaning toilets, bathrooms, kitchens, even cooking functions at home. So (AI) machine-man can reduce housewives works at home. Moreover, (AI) machine man can take care old people , when who are living at homes or elder care centers.

So, it seems artificial intelligence (AI) will be possible developed to manufacture a new generation machine-man to assist (serve) families to do any simply cleaning or cooking jobs at homes. Moreover, the overall demand of (AI) general social needs will also rise, such as security, driving transportation tools, restaurant cleaning, elder centers care service etc. So, it seems that individual or families or social needs of (AI) will be increase in the future. Thus, it will influence macro economy growth (GDP) if there are large house family consumer group and hotel or bus or taxis or ferry etc. different business consumer group demand any artificial intelligence machine numbers increasing. Then, the artificial intelligence products and material manufacturers must need to buy many artificaial intelligence materials to produce any kinds of artificial intelligence machines to prepare to satisfy consumer individual needs. Consequently, macro economy will grow to the owned artificial intelligence development countries, e.g. US, China, UK.

● Why can artificial intelligence satisfy human needs?

First, On machine-man satisfactory demand aspect view point, it makes computers that think, it is the automation of activities. We associate with human thinking: like decision making, learning. It is the act of creating machine that perform function that require intelligence when performed by people. It is the study of mental faculties through the use of computational models. It is the study of computations that make it possible to perceive, reason and act. It is a branch of computer science that is concerned with the automation of intelligent behavior. It is anything in computing service that human don't yet know how to do property.

Second, on thought aspect artificial intelligence means systems thank think like humans, systems that think rationally.

Third, on behavioral aspect, artificial intelligence systems that act like human and that systems act rationally. However, the basic objective of (AI) is to represent human's thought processes in computation . These machines are supposed to exhibit behavior that. It is performed by a human being, would be considered intelligent. However, some authors feel (AI) has disadvantages, such as it is not creative, it is excited in the use of sensory devices, it can't make use of a very wide context of experiences and it does not use common sense.

For speech recognition and understanding function needs example, (AI) can be applied in speech recognition and understanding function, which (AI) speech or voice recognition is a data input method. For example, the computer recognizes and understands one (or a few) word commands. Speech understanding on the other hand is the computer's ability to understanding a spoken language. That is , the computer understands the meaning of sentences, an paragraphs through (AI).

So, (AI) can be attempted to learn human language how to speak. It is similar to translate human language skill, instead of actual human speaking skill. Also, (AI) can assist handicap learning or language student how to listen different languages by machine-man sounds from computers more accurately. So, it seems that it (AI) can replace human language teachers speaking function and can change teaching language nature of job in language speaking and listening education industry.

● Is artificial intelligence one good choicc for human future technological benefit?

Nowadays, new technology development is popular. However, artificial intelligence is one kind of new technology choice among different technologies innovation. So it brings this question: Is artificial intelligence technology value to invest? To answer this question. I shall indicate some other new technology developments to compare (AI) technology development to judge which has urgent needs to achieve human expectation nowadays.

For example, why is green peace interested in new technologies? New technologies features prominently in our ongoing campaigns against genetic modified crops and number power. However, which are also an integral part of our solutions to environmental challenges, including renewable energy technologies, such as solar, wind and wave (water) power energy as well as waste treatment technologies, such as mechanical, biological treatment.

It seems humans need concern how to apply (AI) technology to solve environment pollution challenges in our future. So, environment protective, agriculture, natural energy technology will be popular demand to attempt to apply (AI) technology to solve their challenges or apply (AI) to assist to develop their industry.

What is relationship between
(AI) and economy growth?

● How can artificial intelligence technology influence economy?

Advances in artificial intelligence (AI) technology and related fields have opened up new markets and new opportunities progress in critical areas, such as health, education, energy, economic development, social welfare and the environment pollution.

(AI) automation will continue to create wealth and expand the global economy development in the future. However, when many will benefits that growth won't be costless and will be accompanied by changes in the skills, that workers need to increase productivity in the economy and structural changes in the economy. So, in the skills that workers need to succeed in the economy and structural changes.

I shall indicate why aggressive policy action will be needed to help Americans who are disadvantaged by these changes , due to (AI) technology is caused. For automation industry change example, artificial intelligence (AI) capabilities will enable automation of some tasks that have long required human labor. These artificial intelligence technology introduction can increase new opportunities for individuals. The economy and society, but (AI) has also the potential to disrupt be current livelihoods of many Americans. However, (AI) leads to unemployment and increase in inequality over the long run depends not only on the (AI) technology itself, but also on the institutions and policies that are changed.

Thus, it is possible that (AI) technology will raise some countries unemployment number if the employer apply (AI) technology workers to work instead of human labor in their factories, but it can also raise productivities for these employers.

● Can (AI) influence global economy growth?

Technological progress is main driver of growth of GDP per capita, allowing output to increase faster than labor and capital . However, technology can increase productivity, but also decrease the number of labor hours needed to create a unit of output. So (AI) causes unequal to labor wage decreases, even reduces the number of labor to manufacture, e.g. artificial intelligence technology of automation car manufacturing industry; clothing manufacturing industry; plane manufacturing etc. high technology of artificial intelligence manufacturing method. But (AI) should be potential environment benefit, although it raises unemployment ratio. Moreover, it can rise production , due to many skilled craft were replaced by the combination of machines and lower-skilled labor. The result of (AI) technology introduction , it causes output per hour risen when inequality declined, driving up average living standards, but the labor of some high-skill workers was no longer as valuable in the market. Otherwise, if (AI) technology is continue developed to be success. Some routine intensive occupations will be loss, which focused on predictable, e.g. easily programmable tasks, such as switchboard operators, filing clerks, travel agents, and assembly line workers would be particularly replaced by new (AI) technology. However, at the same time, (AI) technology development will bring these benefits: improvement in education (training (AI) technology scientists) , due to (AI) manufacturing technology needs are raising to businesses and institutional changes, such as the reduction in unionization and raising in the minimum wage to the (AI) manufacturing technology skilled labor in factories.

Because (AI) technology is not a single technology, but rather a collection of technologies that are applied to specific tasks, the effects of (AI) will be felt unevenly though the economy. It will bring some tasks will be most easily automated than others , and some jobs will be affected more than others, both negatively and positively. Finally, new jobs are likely to be directly created in areas , such as the development and supervision of (AI) as well as indirectly created in a range areas though out the economy as higher incomes lead to expanded demand.

However, if (AI) technology could dominate global labor markets. If labor productivity increases, do not influence into wage increases, then the large economic gains brought about by (AI) technology could be increased wealth inequality, due to employers can reduce production cost, but workers (labors) wages will not be increased, even will be decreased. Hence, it seems the (AI) technology will bring disadvantages to labor market to cause unemployment or reduce wages in possible, although it can reduce employer individual salary (wage) expenditure and it can raise productivity.

● How can artificial intelligence impact global economy growth?

Artificial intelligence (AI) technology is a branch of computer science that aims to create intelligent machines that work and react like humans. So, (AI) is a technology that appears to impact (influence) human preference by learning, understanding complex contents, enhancing humans in executing both routine and non-routine tasks. In the future, (AI) technology that can be virtual personal assistant, as well as it may exist, such as robots with human-like processing capabilities.

How can (AI) technology impact global economy growth over the next 10 years? During this time period, (AI) technology is predicted to have wide-ranging applications including: Machine learning that automates analytical model building by using algorithms that allow machines to operate without human assistance.

In global education aspect, potential applications include predicting cause-and-effect relationships from biological data, identifying new drugs, self-driving cars, and protecting against fraud, improved natural language processing that allows computers to continue to better analysis, understand and generate language to interface with humans using natural human languages. For example, transcribing notes dictated by physicians, automatically drafting articles and translating text and speech. So (AI) technology can be applied to education aspect to improve humans' knowledge level.

In visual art aspect, (AI) machine vision that allows computers to identify objects, scenes and activities in images. Current applications of (AI) machine vision include providing objective descriptions for the blind seeing(visual) needs.

We except the economic effects of (AI) technology to include both direct GDP growth from sectors that develop or manufacture. (AI) technology and indirect GDP growth through increased productivity in existing sectors that employ some form of (AI). If (AI) technology is an increasingly critical component of more products, it will become an integral part of many people's lives. Thus, (AI)'s ability to influence economic activity, rather than the economic or development status of the region. (AI) has the potential to impact income classes and to bring significant gains to both developed and developing countries. For example, (AI) has the potential to optimize good production around the world by analyzing agricultural regions and identifying what is necessary to improve crop yields.

In estimating the future economic effects by (AI) technology innovation, it is important to note that it is challenging to accurately predict which applications of (AI) will ultimately be commercially successful. In micro level economic influence, we need to apply methodologies to estimate the economic effects of investment in firms developing (AI) technology since investment levels in a technology are a telling sign of the future potential of that (AI) technology.

● How can (AI) influence GDP of high income countries in the next ten years?

How (AI)'s development may affect the global economy over the next ten years. In fact, (AI) technology has the potential to affect business across the global in a wide range of industries in ways only a number of technologies have done in the parts. For example, (AI) technology's expected to be a useful tool for enhancing human capabilities and in some instances replacing functions, such as driving a car, adoption of broadband internet, mobile telephone, industrial robotic automation have served to enhance human capabilities.

However, significant public debate has focused on projections of (AI) technology's effect on the labor force. However, large companies prefer to invest in (AI) technological industry. For example, face book's (AI) research lab., google machine intelligence lab. and micro soft machine learning and artificial intelligence research division are all making advances in (AI) technology and investing in the industry's top talent. Additionally, between 2010 year and 2015 year, nearly $5 billion in venture capital funding invested in firms across the global developing and employing (AI) technology (Facebook (AI) Research).

● How can artificial intelligence impact on workplace?

Modern information technologies and the labor economy growth of machines is powered by artificial intelligence have already strongly influenced the world of work in the 21 ST century. Computers, algorithms and software simplify every tasks and it is impossible to image how most of our life could be managed without them. How can be the information economy characterized by exponential growth replaces the most production industry based on economy of scales? What will the future world of work look like and how long will it take to get? Will the future world of work be a world where humans spend less time earning their livelihood? Alternatively, are mass unemployment, mass poverty and social distortions also possible scenario for the future, where robots, artificial intelligence systems play an increasingly central role? These questions concern how artificial intelligence further development . Can influence labor economy growth on workplace ? When the labor market has widespread impact on intelligence property, information technology, product liability, competition and labor and employment laws.

How (AI) technology impacts on labor workplace.

The future influence any organizations how labor economies use of (AI) can be analyzed, such as deep machine learning is based on a set of model high level data. Unlike human workers, the machines are connected the whole time in workplace. If one machine makes a mistake, all autonomous systems will keep this in mind and will avoid the same mistake the next time.

Over the long run intelligent machines will win against every human expert. Production robots have been replacing employees because of the (AI) technology. They work more precisely than humans and cost loss. Creative solutions like 3D printers and the self learning ability of these production robots will replace human workers, the automatic data recording and data processing, traditional back office activities are no longer in demand. Autonomous software will collect necessary information and will send it to the employee who needs it. Additionally, dematerialization leads to the phenomenon that traditional physical products are becoming software. For example, CD or DVDs are being replaced by streaming services. The replacement of traditional event ticket, e-travel ticket service products or hard cash will be the next step, due to the possibility of payment by smartphone. So, (AI) technology will impact human's daily life consumption behaviors in the future. For another example, transportation tools, such as boats and ferries and private vehicles will use sensors and navigating without human input. Taxi and truck drivers will become obsolete, the stock store applies to stock managers and postal carriers of the delivery is distributed by (AI) machine delivery method.

What is the relationship between (AI) and (CRM)?
● Can (AI) technology impact on customer relationship management (CRM) ?
Nowadays , (AI) is a technology almost as old as the computer industry itself, it is similar with the advent of personal assistants function to businesses and personal promotion channel, such as (Amazon's Alexa, Apple's Siri, Google's Assistant) image recognition (face book), personalized recommendations (Netflix , Amazon). Those innovations have been driven by a increase in processing power, lower cost hardware, and the exploding creation and availability of data. It seems, (AI) technology can impact global customer service management method.

How to forecast economic impact modeling to (AI) will affect global economy? Can human forecast business revenue growth and job creation (or destruction) based on (AI) applied to customer relationship management (CRM) activities? In addition to the economic impact on (AI) or (CRM) which can include an estimate of the economic impact attributable to sales forces customer base. What can economic benefits be brought to (CRM) from (AI) technology?

Artificial intelligence(AI) comprises a set of technologies that use natural language processing, machine learning, knowledge graphs, and other tools to answer questions, discover insights and provide recommendations. Computer systems can use (AI) hypothesize and formulate possible answers based on available evidence can be trained through the ingestion of vast amounts of content, and automatically adapt and learn from (AI) self mistakes and failures.

So, any business organizations (customer service departments) can provide efficient and effective customer relationship management of excellent customer service quality if which applied (AI) technology system. The different type of (AI) systems include: (AI) system platforms, machine learning (AI) based data preparation and enrichment tools, machine vision/ image recognition, voice speech recognition, text analysis and natural language processing, bots , e.g. face book website and virtual digital assistance solutions, social media pattern analysis , sentiment analysis, advanced numerical analysis (e.g. IOT streaming , machine logs), supporting technologies, knowledge base dialog management, Q&A processing etc. different (AI) technology system customer relationship management (CRM) tools.

(AI) (CRM) of activity can include these categories, such as: corporate marketing, marketing operation, field marketing, customer support, digital commerce, customer analytics, customer influenced product or service design, product or service pricing, finance information, presentation, customer billing, inventory , logistics and fulfilment support, partner management etc. different CRM tools.

(AI) technology of CRM has been carrying on plan different stages to achieve CRM personal assistant tool for businesses. The stages are such as, in the beginning stage of (AI) projects in place, implement now, pilot phase next year in the final stage of (AI) customer relationship management tools are foreseeable future. So, this CRM technology has been improved to plan in different stages every year to prepare to achieve full capacity of CRM service quality for businesses to use in the future.

Hence, how to develop an estimate prediction of the economic impact (AI) technologies could have CRM activities, which depends on gathering macroeconomic information on business revenue and the basic marketing of business revenue and the basic markup of business expenses by major functions (customer support, marketing and sales , production etc.)

An economic impact model that can gather data together and forecast the results how (AI) artificial intelligence technology brings (CRM) customer relationship management benefits to businesses, e.g. surveys investigation includes IT spending by sample countries, GDP and population estimates and forecasts, revenue per employee and ratios of IT spend to GDP. Surveys (questionnaire questions) of forecast results are influenced by (AI) impact can include: results are projected from surveys and rely on estimates are made by respondents on the expected financial improvements in categories of (AI) –assisted customer relationship management activities. The forecast assumes that these estimates are correct; financial estimates are based on estimates of "first year" improvement from full (AI) implementation; forecasts are from planning to implement any artificial intelligence of customer relationship management (CRM) projects, the improvement forecast is of categories of activity , e.g. corporate marketing , digital commerce, and customer analytics. They are not estimates of ROI for the

(AI) software. They rely on conservative estimates to which each of these entities might affect company revenue, expenses or productivity. They also rely on estimates of the penetration of software in customer relationship management activities . Net new jobs created are based on the ratio of new revenue to jobs required to support that revenue . They can assume that 50% of the net new revenue will support increases in labor and the rest will go for capital and other operating expenses that may replace jobs lost to automation.

In the future, some of the ways in micro economic benefits to any organizations. (AI) technology is expected to impact CRM activities include: Spending up sales cycles, improving lead generation and qualification solving customer support problems faster (raising service quality), helping companies improve brand campaigns and recognition, lowering costs of support calls when increasing resolution rates, lowering the cost of recruiting employees and partners, increasing revenue from optimized product marketing, optimizing price, distribution logistics and preventing loss through fraud detection. So, micro economic benefits view point, it seems that (AI) CRM technology can raise any companies economic benefits for care term.

Artificial intelligence enables machines or the in-build software to behave like human beings which allows these decisions and act. The advent of (AI) is leading , talking, making decisions and act. The advent of (AI) is leading to new technologies advances and transforming the economic and employment opportunities for humans in a positive way. (AI) related technologies can facilitate our live. For example, industrial robotics, robotic medical assistants, smart games, financial forecasting software, big data analysis, algorithms in health and bioinformatics, pilotless cargo places, drone ambulances and general purpose and workplace robots and others. (Disruptors technologies: Advances that will transform life, business and the global economy).

Artificial intelligence also known as computational intelligence is defined as " the human –like intelligence exhibited by machines or software. It is theorized that intelligence of humans can be described and intelligence machines or software can simulate it. These machines software can be reasonable , learn, perceive and process information, like human mind and thus facilitate human life. They can think and act for us. So, artificial intelligence is an interdisciplinary field of study including computer science, neuroscience, psychology, linguistics and philosophy.

However, (AI) research and developments have economically impacted many industries, such as robotics, telecommunications, computer applications , health, finance, heavy manufacturing, transportation, aviation, e-service and e-commerce, military , music and movie, toys and games entertainment etc. industries.

In fact, many ideas, systems and technologies have been developing in the world of (AI) technology. However, which are net called or considered (AI) products, rather which are mentioned with their specific names, such as smart graphics, machine learning, e-commerce etc. (i.e. this is called (AI) effect).

What is relationship between
(AI) and digital economy?

● How can (AI) technology influence digital economy?
Nowadays, (AI) related industrial applications will replace most human power in fields, including call centers, customer services and air cargo transportation. (AI) technologies also help weather forecasting based on repeated rainfall pattern (data) recognition, through robotics (i.e. floor cleaning, moving lawns etc.) transporting people and products with unmanned vehicles, sending space unmanned smart shuttles, developing robotic arms, predicting market values in stock exchanges by internet, making homes safer, helping elderly and disabled using robotic servants etc.

Among the (AI) related technologies , there are a few that significance for the impact on society and especially on digital economy . (AI) is particularly influential in machine learning. Such as robotics, transportation, finance, health and bioinformatics, e-commerce , e-games, big online data gathering and internet-of-things. For example, machine e-learning is based in bioinformatics and robots that can learn new skills for better caregiving in healthcare. What is machine e-learning? Machines can e-learn from e-data gathering, coming up generalizations and making decisions to act in certain ways from internet.

There are important applications , such as e-machine perception, electronic online natural language learning processing, online search engines, online bioinformatics, online brain –computer interface, online game playing, online robot locomotion, online advertising, online computations finances, online health monitoring, online DNA classification and decision making, online in chemistry –cheminformatics . So, online machine learning can positively impact productivity and it can enhance information and analytical system from (AI) online channel.

What is robotics? Robotics is one of the most strongly influenced fields in (AI). For example, heavy manufacturing industries, robots and used and man power is replaced for effectiveness, precision, and accuracy, especially in respective or dangerous tasks, including welding, assembling , picking and placing .

So, robots can acquire new skills or adapt the changing dynamic environment. Also, artificial intelligence can be applied in developing transportation. For example, automated vehicles, driver assistance systems , safety systems, collision avoidance systems and public transportation. Moreover, (AI) technology has proven to produce some of the best tools to predict stock market fluctuations from internet data gathering method. It's predictions are based on ever-evolving predictions algorithms and systems learn new models and make connections between historical data and new data to measure stock market trading more accurate from internet data gathering channel.

In health field, especially in health data processing , analysis, decision making support and medical diagnosis. So, online data can show which patients will need what treatment and what alternative drugs could be used more accurate from (AI) online data gathering method. Bioinformatics is an interdisciplinary field combining statistics, (AI) online technology can help in discovering data patterns and modeling through the application of machine learning, artificial neural networks and genetic algorithms. For example, further (AI) technology development of human genome project of online data sequences.

Online shopping can be facilitated by virtual assistants developed through (AI) technology and these assistants can offer the best advice. (AI) online purchase coming after every product image recommendations and personalization bring important revenue to shopping online sites, like Amazon . Smart computer graphics and games, artificial intelligence is useful in smarter computer, graphics, scene modeling , scene rendering processes in order to create, for example, effective human −robot interactions , online machine learning, online strategic games techniques etc. online computer related (AI) software.

So, online big data analysis and big data does have a critical need in the world of online intelligence machines and software in our future. In other words, (AI) offers online technology to enable online big data analysis to provide industrial organizations with valuable information for effective decision making in short time. For example, what IBM's Watson achieved: this machine used 200 million of structured and unstructured content with a special technology of hypothesis generation, massive evidence gathering, analysis and scoring from internet channel.

Finally, (AI) online technology another related internet invention (internet of things) (IOT) is the network of machines or objects connected through internet. These connected objects can sense their internal and external environment, communicate with each other, can send critical data and finally can make decisions to act or correct their environment from (AI) online technology. For example, factories can monitor and automatically change production processes, hospitals can monitor and regulate the health conditions of their patients , schools can collect data from facilities and cars can send data to car makers from (AI) online technology.

Partner predicts that (IOT) market will create about trillion amount value by 2020 year. Although machines collect big data from their environment, whether which gain an insight or learn from these online data largely depends on the (AI) online machine learning principals and (AI) online technology. In 2013, Mckinsey estimated that disruptive technologies closely related with potential economic impact in 2025 year between $7.1 to $13.1 trillion amount (automation of knowledge work, advanced robotics, autonomous or near-autonomous vehicles).

What is the relationship between
(AI) and global digital economy development ?

● Could work activities in China be automated
making in the nation with the world's largest automation potential?
Can (AI) technology influence China economy? Could China workers be affected and jobs made up of routine work activities and predictable? Will programmable tasks be particularly impact to China employment market ? When impact on labor market is likely to be gradual at the aggregate level, it can be sudden and dramatic at the level of specific work activities, rending some job obsolete fairly. Overall (AI) technology will raise digital skills when reducing demand for medium incomer inequality for China workers. It seems (AI) technology's effect on productivity could be crucial to China's future economic growth as the population ages are increasing.
In China, some biggest technological companies driving significant investments in research and development. Moreover, China is one of the

leading global (AI) technology development county. However, China will need to focus on building its innovation capacity. For example, United States and United Kingdom are currently producing more influential (AI) technological research. However, if China planed to achieve (AI) technology success, it's traditional industries will need to develop technical know-how –to and overcoming implementation costs prepare to develop (AI) . When (AI) technology is introduced into China society, China government needs to raise concerning ethical, legal, technological security etc. business questions. Also, surrounding issues include privacy, discrimination, legal liability and regulation. It aims to encourage overseas investors to choose to invest (AI) technological industry to raise GDP growth and manufacturing industries income growth for long term in China. If China encouraged overseas (AI) technology investment in its country. It is possible to influence China employment market to be changed. Because (AI) technology will impact to influence China people daily life. Due to (AI) technology is introduced to China society, many rich people will prefer to spend to buy any high (AI) technological products for entertainment or learning or machine man driving etc. daily necessity activities. Then it will raise GDP growth and will raise (AI) manufacturers or related-(AI) technological manufacturers profit. It is beneficial to China because it can become one high knowledgeable and (AI) technological economical society. But it will bring bad influences to raise unemployment chance for the low skillful labor. In labor economy aspect influence , how (AI) technology can influence China low skillful labor unemployment ratio raising. The raising low skill labor unemployment reason is because China low skillful human labors are argued or are replaced by (AI) technology creating new challenges to introduce to influence China society of simply human manufacturing job nature to be changed to be high (AI) technology manufacturing job nature in any China factories. Moreover, when (AI) technology introduction to China, it will cause other related social challenges in China. The varied (AI) related challenges, including the difficulty of creating safe and reliable hardware for sensing and affecting (transportation and education), the challenges of gaining public trust, a low resource comities and public safety and security, the challenges of overcoming fears or marginalizing humans in China employment and workplace and the risk of diminishing interpersonal trust because the low skillful labors won't believe any China employers will give chance to employ them , due to (AI) technology will replace their skills and man manufacturing of productivity is much less to compare to (AI) technology manufacturing method.

● How does (AI) technology influence
the future of employment change?

Are future nature of jobs changed to computerization from (AI) technology? Where are the probability of computing occupations from (AI) technology influence? What is expected impacts of future computing on labor market from (AI) technology influence? John Maynard Keynes's frequently cited prediction of widespread technological unemployment " du to our discovery of means of economic the use of labor outrunning the pace of which we can find new used of labor" (Keynes, 1933, p.3).

In the future, (AI) technology will impact some nature of occupations to change computing. This chance will also influence some countries' economic change. For example, some factory human labors hand routine manufacturing tasks will be changed to computerization of routine manufacturing tasks by (AI) technological machine men hand manufacturing method. it will cause a structured shift in the labor market, with workers reallocating their labor supply from middle-income manufacturing to low-income service occupations.

Arguably, this is because the manual tasks of service occupations are less computerization, as who require a higher degree of flexibility and physical adaptability. So, (AI) technology will influence the human hand labor skillful occupation nature of task cheaper , such as vehicle manufacturing , ship manufacturing, computer manufacturing, steel manufacturing, television, radio etc. home electronic products of heavy machine industry change. Due to (AI) technology machine man will be proper to be used to manufacturing these electronic products when the (AI) technology innovation can develop to the mature stage. Then, any countries manufacturers will choose to use (AI) technology machine man, instead of human hand production.

Supposing the future prices of computing are fallen, seriously, problem solving skills are becoming relatively productive, explaining the substantial employment growth in manufacturing occupations, involving cognitive tasks where skilled labor has a comparative advantage, as well as the increase education needs for (AI) technology computing of machine man subject study.

Prediction of education needs for (AI) technology student numbers will increase, due to manufacturing industry needs many (AI) technology students in future employment market. Another (AI) technology influence if the future (AI) technological innovation, e.g. machine man manufacturing or machine man service industries will both increase demand, then with more sophistic software technologies will be disrupted labor markets by marketing workers redundant.

For publishing industry, what is striking about the case in paper book publishing industry will be unpopular? Due to the electronic book publishing industry will be popular, e.g. Amazon publish . (AI) technology can influence paper book manufacturing method which is replaced by machine man electronic book manufacturing method as well as it will cause the computerization is no longer confined to routine manufacturing tasks. Due to (AI) machine man manufacturing technology will be proper to be used to manufacture any products in short time efficiently and effectively , e.g. electronic book products. In the future, if it is fact to occur this case, such as (AI) technological machine man manufacturing method will be adopted (applied) to manufacture electronic books or any products in possible. (AI) technology will cause many manufacturing workers are unemployed. It is beneficial to employers, who can reduce to spend much wages expenditure to employ manufacturing workers, but it will cause many manufacturing workers loss jobs and reduce income to support whose families lives. It will cause social challenges, e.g. increasing stealing crimes if the manufacturing workers had not other skills to find other jobs to do easily. So, manufacturers need to concern over technological unemployment which will be hardly future phenomenon if who decided to dismiss all manufacturing workers, due to (AI) technology machine men replace to them.

If (AI) technology can be innovated to produce any kinds of machine man to serve any service or manufacturing industries successfully. Then, it will bring these questions: Can future that workers be influenced to be automation employment and productivity by (AI) technology influence? Does it impact to influence the (AI) technology countries' productivity and growth and natural resources development and labor markets and evolution of global financial markets and economic impact of technology and innovation and urbanization etc. issues? How will automation transform the workplace? What will be the implication for employment? What is likely to be its impact both on productivity in the global economy and on employment?

In fact, automatic of activities can enable businesses to improve performance by reducing errors chance and improving quality and speed, and same cases achieving outcomes that go beyond human capabilities. Some economists indicate (AI) technology would give a needed boost to economic growth and prosperity have of the working age population in many countries. Based on the scenario modeling, they estimate automation could raise productivity growth globally by 0.8 to 1.4 % annually. They also indicated that almost half the activities people are almost $1.6 trillion in wages to do in the global economy have the potential to be automated adapting current demonstrates technology, according to their analysis of more than 2,000 work activities across 800 occupations. When less than 5% of all occupations can be automated entirely using demonstrated technology, about 60% of all occupations have at least 30% of worker made activities, that would be automated. More occupation will change to be automated. They also indicated for business performance benefits of automation are relatively clear, but the issues are more complicated by policy making to attract foreign investors. Beyond technical feasibility, the cost of technology, competition labor will include skills and supply and demand dynamics, performance benefits and beyond labor cost savings and social and regulatory acceptance will affect the automation. Their predictions suggest that half of today work activities could be automated by 2055 year, but this could happen 10 to 20 years earlier or latter depending on the various factors in addition to their wider economic condition.

Some scientists suggest (AI) technology is finally starting to deliver real-life business benefits. Computer power is growing significantly , algorithms are becoming more sophisticated and perhaps most important of all, the world is generating vast quantities of the fuel that powers (AI) technology data billions of gigabytes of it every day. Also, online firms are digital natives, such as Google online search service company is investing on (AI) technology. For new though most of the news if coming from the suppliers of (AI) technologies. And many new users are only in the experimental phase. Few products are on the market or are likely to arrive these soon to drive immediate and widespread adoption. As a result, analysts believe (AI) technology's potential will give true economic benefit in the future. (AI) industry will introduce to suppliers and users to raise economic potential of (AI) technology.

In the future, (AI) technology systems can solve business problems. Some scientists categorized those into five technology systems that are key areas of (AI) technology development: robotics and autonomous vehicles, computer vision language virtual agents and machine learning , which is based on algorithms that learn from data without replying on rules-based programming in order to draw conclusions or direct an action.

Such as computer vision and language includes natural language processing, analytics, speech recognition technology, some are about learning from information, such as about machine learning and others are related to acting on information, such as robotics, autonomous vehicles and virtual agents, which are computer programs that can converse with humans. Machine learning and a subfield called deep learning are artificial intelligence applications.

- Can artificial intelligence impact
global economy growth?

Artificial intelligence (AI) is a term first defined in 1956 year. It is a branch of computer science that aims to create intelligent machines that work and react like humans. In contrast today, 60 years later, (AI) is characterized by a number of applications, including computers playing games against humans and understanding human languages, virtual personal assistants, and robotics which involve computers seeing , hearing and reacting to sensory stimuli. In the future, technologists predict for (AI) technology ranging from (AI) being used as a tool to aid relatively simple processes for robots with human like mental capabilities, who expect (AI) technology can emulate human performance by learning, coming to mind its own conclusions, understanding complex content, engaging in dialog with people, enhancing human cognitive performance or replacing humans in executing both routine and non-routine tasks. In existing industry, (AI) technology is used , such as targeted advertising and virtual used personal assistant as well as the (AI) technology that my exist in the future, such as robots with human vehicle processing capabilities.

The range of (AI) technology's progress in the future will determine the economic impact future of (AI) technology on the global economy with more limited advances and applications (i.e. weak (AI) only) corresponding to more limited economic impacts and more substantial progress, i.e. strong (AI) technology is corresponding to more significant economic impact.

(AI) technology learning that automates analytical model, including predicting cause-and-effect relationship from biological data, identifying new drugs, self-driving cars and protecting against fraud etc. functions. Also (AI) learning can improve natural language processing that allows computers to continue to better analyze, understand and generate language to interface with human using the natural human language, virtual personal assistant, helps users by providing scheduling appointment, reminds organizing personal finance and finding providers of various services, machine vision allows (AI) machine man to identify object, scenes and activities in detect pedestrians and bicyclists.

We expect the economic effects of (AI) technology to include both direct GDP growth from sectors that develop or manufacture (AI) technology and indirect GDP growth through increased productivity in existing sectors that employ some from of (AI) technology. If (AI) producing sectors could grow, then it could lead to increase revenues and employment of (AI) technological professionals within these existing firms as well as the potential creation of entirely new economic activities to any countries' societies productivity improvement in existing sectors could be realized through faster and move efficient processes and decision making as well as increased (AI) technological knowledge and access to information available in societies easily.

In the future, if (AI) technology is an increasingly critical component of more products, it will become an integral part of necessary products of many people's lives. The extent of (AI)'s economy effort is also likely to vary from region to region, thought variation may be more dependent on the predominate economic activity of a region and the (AI) ability can influence economic activity, rather then the economic or developmental status of the regions. (AI) technology can move accessibility and can use source development to do international business between one country and another country.

So (AI) technology has the potential to give benefits to different income chooses and to bring significant gains to both developed and developing countries. For agricultural technology, (AI) has the potential to optimize food production around the world by analyzing agricultural regions and identifying what is necessary to improve crop yield. In total, (AI) technology gives greater economic impact to any countries agricultural regions if which implemented (AI) technology to grow crop , fruit etc. food production in the farms.

Investment in (AI) technology is such as capital investment to any countries' public or private enterprises. So, it will have large economic impact to the future . If the (AI) technology is reasonable invested to the different needs aspect by the public or private enterprises in the country.

Then, it will have good economic impact to the country in the future. However, when (AI) technology is likely to affect both the productivity and employment components of economic growth in many sectors. Significant public debate has focused on projections of (AI)'s effect on the labor force. However, for instance, some researchers have argued that the rise of (AI) technology and automation will led to significant unemployment as capital is substituted for the low skillful labor. So, they point to the concern that the increasing sophistication of (AI) technology may balance skilled and semi-skilled workers and the reduce the size of the middle class. However, this is not a new argument, due to (AI) technology negatively affecting the labor force and leading to mass unemployment. Because the (AI) technology is the substitution of machinery for human labor. Although, employment in certain industries, has been reduced in the past due to technological advancement. For long term, the labor market has adapted to the introduction of new technology, giving rise to new jobs in new areas. (AI) technology may also be accomplished without a reduction to total employment in the long-term to some Asia countries, such as Hong Kong and Japan. Because Hong Kong and Japan many low skilled labor, e.g. security, cleaner who complaint that employers need them to work long time hours. (abnormal working hours) e.g. one day 12 to 15 working hour per day. Hence, if (AI) machine means invention technology success. Security or cleaning job can be worked from (AI) machine man in some hours every day in order to reduce the long time working hours cleaners or security workers, e.g. one (AI) machine man works 4 hours for cleaning or security job, one day as well as another cleaner or security labor only needs to work 8 hours one day. So total security or cleaning employers can employ 12 hours machine cleaners or security workers and human cleaners or security workers in one day. For long term benefit, Hong Kong or Japan every security or cleaning worker does not need to work 12 hours minimum working hours one day. They won't feel tried and bore and without private with whose families, so who will accept to do these cleaning or security jobs, even they can raise work efficient and performance when who feel happy and health.

So, (AI) technology of machine man invention can raise low skillful labor efficiency and it can help them to avoid abnormal working hours demand in some busy work life countries, such as Hong Kong and Japan. Before, one Japan female labor feel unhappy to work, due to who often needs to work abnormal working hours for her employer and who has less sleeping and without any private time to enjoy her life with her families every day. So this abnormal working hours factor causes her to do commit suicide behavior, then she is die unlucky. So (AI) technology of machine man invention ought avoid abnormal working hours demand for employer in any countries in the future.

The most important occurrence to any employers, some researchers had attempted to do one experiment to find that private research and development , venture capital and public research and development investment all have strong net effect or economic growth with venture capital funding further having the strongest such effect from (AI) technology. The researchers hypothesize the venture capital investment contributes to economic growth through (AI) technology innovation and by the capacity of an economy to use existing (AI) technology knowledge to increase productivity. They predict the impacts of venture capital, business-research and development and public research and development can raise multi factor productivity from (AI) technology introduction.

Can (AI) technology influence the economic development to developing countries? The developing regions of the world contain most of natural resources. If one day, (AI) technology has invent one kind of machine man which can assist any gas or oil workers to seek any new oil/gas natural resource locations easily. I believe that (AI) technology can help these natural resource exploitation countries will gain economic benefit more easily. So, (AI) driven technology can be used to change to create any new opportunities to address poor management or resources and improve human well being, such as Africa Latin America and India can use (AI) technology machine man to seek any oil/gas natural resource countries exploitation activities to attempt to gain much economic benefits.

● Why will (AI) technology grow economic development ?

Nowadays, increases in capital and labor are no longer driving the levels of economic growth, such as (AI) technology. The ability of increase in capital investment and in labor of traditional drivers of production, have no longer to be enjoyed in most developed economies ,e.g. developed country, US, UK . However, artificial intelligence has the potential to overcome the physical limitation of capital and labor to avoid missing out on this opportunity. So, policy makers and business leaders must prepare for and work toward a future with artificial intelligence. They must do with the idea that (AI) is another simply method to enhance productivity method . Rather they must see (AI) as the tool that can transform thinking about how growth is created.

Economists have always thought of new technologies are as driving growth their ability to enhancing. It can replace labor and capital factor of production. So, it brings this question: What is the factor of production (AI) technology characteristics. They key factor is to see (AI) technology as a capital-labor .

(AI) can replicate labor activities at much greater scale and speed, and to even perform some tasks began the capabilities of human. For example, by using virtual assistants , 1000 legal documents can be reviewed in a matter of days instead of taking three people six moths to complete. Some (AI) technology may be one kind of factor of production in the future. For another example, people will work in workplace digitalization environment. So, in the future, working environment and information management are automated. Such as Konica camera sale company will use workplace digitalization. So , (AI) technology can provide workplace digitalization in order to raise productivity efficiency. (AI) technology will be one kind of production which is replaced by workplace digitalization and it will grow any organization productivity efficiently. Then, (AI) technology will assist overall social economy growth , due to productivity is raised and products can be produced in short time to prepare to sell in consumption market. So, time will be shortened to increase GDP growth fast for the development of (AI) technology countries.

● How can (AI) technology impact to global
economic and social and psychological
changes?

What will be the development of (AI) technology and predictions concerning the future evolution? The computers and robots will develop conscious, intelligent and minds into humans, enhancing psychological and behavioral abilities and allowing for direct communication with (AI) minds. (AI) technology will be impacted human life by (AI) technology information communicative and environmental influence. A " world brain" and " world mind", this psychological system will be enhanced and enriched the capacities of both individual and collective cognition by (AI) technology of service industries.

(AI) technology with influence these human needs of service industries changes, such as , biological science, finance, entertainment, business, biological science, transportation, communication military etc. The personal computer evolution, the internet and the world wide web which exploded on the scene, linking business, homes, schools, social organizations which were a completely unpredicted phenomenon to influence human life. Kurzweil (1999) predicts that by 2029 year, most human communication will be with machines. According to Person, by 2100 year, there will be human machine convergence.

How can (AI) technology influence environmental protection to make benefits to farming economic growth? (AI) technology can be applied to predict how to solve environmental pollution challenge to avoid to damage any crop or vegetable or rice or fruit etc. food growth. Because environmental experts can gather global environmental pollution data from an environmental database to build a perform a systematic analysis from (AI) technology. The first step is this broad analysis can include understanding, statistical and data gathering techniques to obtain the relevant data, the correlation among the variables involved, and a list of possible models. The next step is to select a set of methods and models that cover all kinds of knowledge and functionalities needed for the decision making process. Once the models are selected, they must be fully implemented by means of machine learning , data mining, statistical or numerical technique. After that, those models must be integrated to build the whole EDSS. The EDSS must be tested to check its performance, accuracy, usefulness and reliability, both from the user's and (AI) technology/computer scientist's point of view. If these is any wrong feature in any development stage, such as model's integration, models' implementation, selection of models, database, problem analysis etc. the developers must come back in the update th required components. When the evaluation phase is all right, the EDSS is ready to be applied to the environment. The great contribution of artificial intelligence to EDSS the integration of several methods complementing the classical statistical models/simulation , statistical analysis, linear models, etc. and numerical models (control algorithms, optimization techniques etc.) .

This cooperation makes the resulting systems more reliable and powerful in coping with real world environment systems. Date interpretation has been a principal area of research in (AI) technology since the very beginning. The most demanding problem in the environmental assessment context. Knowledge representation permits the definition of the different types of data that the existing methods adapt to the process. There is also a lot of work to clean, repair and transform the huge available quantities of raw data. Apart from this, the availability of meta-information or background knowledge is required to guide the process. Data mining is multi-disciplinary: It covers expert systems, data based technology, statistics, data visualization and unsupervised machine learning. These techniques operate at the level of data and background information, where numerous and often incompatible new commensurate pieces of information from disparate sources have to be brought together (K, Fedra, 1994).

So, it seems that in the future, (AI) technology with the increasing maturity in particular those related to knowledge and engineering, new dimensions can be assisted to users in environmental decision making are available. For example, many environmental systems are characterized both by incomplete models and by limited data. Hence, in the future, (AI) technology will be applied to predict climate change to reduce crop or fruit etc. food agriculture challenge by climate change bad influence.

● Will (AI) technology influence digital economy change to manufacturing industry ?

To understand how the manufacturing business must adapt to prosper in the technology, we need to understand how (AI) technology will change us to shape our daily habits to satisfy our expectation of products to how we shop and even the immediate of the entire process. For example, taxi services are in the crosshairs as on demand transportation services like, available of the touch of a smart phone button expand. In fact, Yellow lab, US country , san Francisco city's largest taxi company is filing for bankruptcy as the industry starts to change faster than almost anyone expected. However, at this point, its more than an app that is changing, some our taxi passengers renting taxi transportation to catch consumption behavior.

(AI) technology will influence digital economy for taxi passenger's individual customer experience, offering a growing renting taxi to catch of service and feedback opportunities when any one taxi passenger who chooses to use mobile phone app online tool to prepaid to rent any taxi more easily.

Also in the long term, (AI) technology can influence vehicles drive themselves of behavior. Already, companies like Google and GM are working on projects to bring fleets of autonomous vehicles to cities at the path of a button.

Moreover, this on-demand service model is beginning to appear across a much broader range of markets. For example , Amazon company is investing in its own fleet of trucks, planes and even drone at the same time as it pushes for same-day delivery of products. As some point, vehicles will be autonomous too. So, it seems that (AI) technique will influence any transportations choose to use digital autonomous driving technology in the future . For Amazon company case, it is not stopping of logistics. It is also aiming to automatically manage the supply of consumer home products with its recently launched Amazon replenishment service, Dash. Dash is a digital service that enables that connected derive to automatically order physical products from Amazon when supplies are running low. So, it seems (AI) technology will be applied to logistic function by digital technology method introduction in the future.

Hence autonomous vehicles will optimize industry supply chains and logistics operations through increased efficiency and flexibility. In fact, fully automated and lean supply chains will keep reduce load sizes and inventory by leveraging smart distribution technologies and smaller autonomous vehicles by machine man assistance. If Amazon continues to grow market share for online sales by reducing effort required by the consumer to place an order, when also contributing the almost immediate delivery of products to the doorstep. So, it will further fuel the trend toward on-demand derive. As Amazon company fuels the on-demand economy, consumers will expect immediacy in more parts of the digital economy. On top of speed, consumers increasing expect more personalization options.

So, (AI) technology will influence digital manufacturing, such as Amazon publishing to monitor every aspect of every process in real -time and communicating to self-optimized deep learning robotics, new methods of high volume and high customization will become possible. Then, as products merge into product platforms and even services, manufacturers have the opportunity to provide components and platforms used by smaller players. So, (AI) technology will influence manufacturing industry to choose automated SMI lines, robots installed, automation engineers.

Another future (AI) technology development can be applied to space science aspect, such as Automation engineering space in manufacturing process to achieve digital manufacturing benefits to any businesses in the future. Such as reducing cost, shortening manufacturing time, raising efficiency, shortening delivery products to client individual time. How can artificial intelligence give the need and advanced fast and evaluation methods benefits for space exploration? When US NASA (space exploration organization) achieves any space exploration missions, it will answer this question:

When is it useful to have a machine use (AI) technology to achieve a decision? After all, after millions of years of space exploration and rough 10,000 years of civilization, humans are usually quite good at making decisions in complex uncertain environments. Through, Johns Hoplains University's Applied Physical Lab. Research in (AI) technology enabled systems, which has identified three general use cases for (AI) technology to explore space mission:

First, for some tasks (AI) technology is more cost effectiveness than human. Second, (AI) technology is better suited than humans at solving some, but not all problems. Third, (AI) technology allows NASA organization's space exploration mission to develop machines that ate capable of responding faster than when a human is in the decision loop (D. Scheidt, 2012, A. Castano et. al. 2008).

So, the use of (AI) technology to enable science by observing the pace of rapidly evolving phenomena was demonstrated. It is more effectively coordinating and (AI) technology utilizing to earn economic benefits to use for space exploration mission.

However, (AI) technology also have current risk for space exploration. Today (AI) technology is immature and requires further development to reach its potential. For instance, the (AI) technology algorithms that detected the dust derive could not have identified whether the Martain weather represented a threat to the cover. Also it can not yet use instrument input to determine what, where and how to autonomously make the next space science measurement. An equally important factor limiting (AI)'s deployment is that lacks the methodology and technology to effectively test (AI) technology. So, the challenge will testing (AI) enabled system is how (AI) performance can be measured. It would be NASA organization's difficulty to find (AI) technology to develop to carry on researching any space exploration missions in the future. However, (AI) technology will be a good economic benefit choice for space exploration mission in the future.

- What is artificial intelligence potential

benefits and ethical considerations?

The ability of (AI) technology systems to transform vast amounts of complex information into insight has the potential to help solve manufacturing or service challenges for human needs. However, to reap the societal benefits of (AI) systems, humans will need to trust then and make sure that which follow the same ethical principles, moral values, professional codes and social norms that we humans would follow in the same scenario, research and educational efforts as well as carefully designed regulation in order to achieve the most effort of economic benefits goals. For example, international business machines corporation (IBM) is actively engaged both competitors , in global discussions about how to make (AI) ethical and as beneficial as possible for people as social economic benefits.

(AI) is usually defined as the " capability of a computer program to perform tasks or reasoning processes " that human usually associate to intelligence in a human being. Often, it has to do with the ability to make a good decision, even when there is uncertainty, too much information to handle. As an example, play chess or complex card games of entertainment activities is believed to need some form of intelligence in a human being, as well as choosing the best medical facilities in a difficult medical case, or creating something new, such as mathematical theorem or even some form of act, or even driving automatic machine man (self driving vehicle) replacing human driving in the middle of a crowded city.

(AI) needs depends on what we consider being intelligence in the behavior of a human being act a certain point in time. If human belief about human intelligence changes and we don't believe any longer that a certain task requires intelligence, then a computer program performing that task is no longer part of (AI), it becomes just another boring computer program. So, it means that (AI) technology will replace some old computer programs, if human can invent new generation of (AI) software for any functions or activities to satisfy human needs.

As IBM, it argues intelligence. This means that we aim to build systems that enhance and scale human expertise and skills rather than replacing them. We therefore focus on practical applications of (AI) capabilities that assist people in performing well-defined tasks of needs by exploiting and wide range of (AI)-based services. We also use the term " cognitive computing" it is mean a comprehensive net of capabilities based on technology. It comprises the fields of machine learning, reasoning and decision technologies, language, speech and vision recognition and processing technologies, high performance and high efficient functions for any industries or individual consumers needs. For example, robotics, which are usually very good at doing what which are supposed to in any environment, much have public shopping center, factory etc. places which need simply services from the robot (machine man), such as cleans the floor of our houses to the robot that can work together with humans in production chains, passing through the warehouse, robots can take care of the tasks of an entire warehouse and the companion robots like Nao, Pepper, Aibo and Giraff, who can entertain use, talk to use and help elderly people to stay connected to their friends, relatives and doctors.

Google company is building automatic machine (self-driving cars) and has acquired more than 10 robotics companies. Facebook had opened whole new research facility only on (AI) research. Apply computer has developed Siri. Microsoft computer company has built a similar personalized assistant. Google has Deep mind, a UK company whose long term aim is to build general (AI) and has already great potential to win game to the world champion and IBM is investing a huge amount of resources in applying its Watson cognitive computing system to the medical domains to finance and to personalized education. In Europe, IBM is establishing new centers in Munich and Milan focused in the application of cognitive computer capabilities to the internet of things and healthcare respectively.

For example, automatic machine man (self-driving cars) are all about (AI), which used to be able to see what happens in the street (signals ,lanes, other cars, pedestrians, traffic lights, which need to able predict what other cars and pedestrians will do, and who need to be able to cope with unforeseen situations. Since, most car accidents are due to human fault, it is estimated that the adoption of self-driving cars will save about half of the lives that are usually last in car accidents.

IBM Watson company has to understand spoken language, make sense of massive amount to text , respond correctly to questions in many categories, as well as assess its own confidence in responding to such questions. In the future, (AI) technology can own question/answering capabilities that would be very useful, for example, in assisting a doctor when trying to some to the correct diagnosis for a patient and to propose the best therapy .

Intelligent machines can also rely on huge amounts of data to be used to learn how to make better decisions. This data comes from all of us over the years Facebook users have uploaded more than 250 billion pictures and every day who upload about 350 million more. Every second, we submit 40,000 google search queries. So, (AI) technology will be connected through the web from appliances to traffic lights from cars to watches. Other tasks that are very easy for humans are physical and manipulation tasks, such as walking , running, picking up an object to make its shape and location, restricted environment. But (AI) machine man technology still not able to have the general physical and manipulation capabilities even of a 6 year old.

So, it brings this question: Why do (AI) scientists need to concern ethics? Because (AI) technology is complex, information into insight has the potential to reveal long held secrets and help solve some of the world's most difficult problems. (AI) systems can potentially be used to help discover insights to treat disease, predict the whether, and manage the global economy. So, ethic issues is important to and (AI) scientists . If any one new (AI) technology research investigation could success, it will be a secret to and the (AI) scientists can not permit to their loyalty to any competitors to damage the fair (AI) technology products trading market. The country (countries) (AI) technology scientists need to concern ethic issues, who need to keep secrets for their countries economic or/and social benefits. This is moral issues to any countries/country loyalty is whose countries intangible assets. They can not sell (AI) loyalty to any their countries to assist whose economic benefits immorally.

● How can (AI) technology influence to global health care economy development?

According to (AI) lecturer analysis, when combined key clinical health (AI) application can potentially create $150 billion in annual savings for the US healthcare economy by 2026 year. (AI) technology is re-winning modern conception of healthcare delivery. It enables machines to sense, comprehend, act and learn. So which can perform administrative and clinical healthcare functions (Accenture, 2017).

It will help health care service organizations to reduce health care cost, will improve and raise service quality and access. So, (AI) health market size will be predicted growth. (AI) applications in health care include robot-assisted surgery, virtual nursing assistant, administrative workflow assistant, fraud detection, error reduction connected machines, clinical trial participant identifier, preliminary diagnosis, automated image diagnosis and cybersecurity.

What kind of benefits (AI) technology can contribute to healthcare service? (AI) technology can deliver what many health care organizations need, such as financial and operational of labor costs, digital expectations from patient consumers how to use (AI) technology to solve interoperability challenges in any healthcare organizations. Also (AI) technology can be applied to wellness an d lifestyle management, diagnostics, delivers financially but also way of organizational and workflow improvement. So, (AI) technology will be continue to become most prevalent and adoption to healthcare organizations , which must need to enhance structure to be position to take full advantages of new (AI) technological capabilities. (AI) technology can change the nature of work and employment is rapidly changing to make the best use of both humans and (AI) talent in healthcare industry in the future. For example, (AI) technology offers a way to fill in gaps and the rising labor shortage in healthcare. According to Accenture analysis, the physicians shortage is increasing. However, (AI) technology will manufacture healthcare machine men to replace physicians in future one day(2017). Hence, (AI) technology will be invented to raise health care service staffs work efficiency and performance in any hospitals or clinics in the future.

In conclusion, (AI) technology will raise efficiency for any service or manufacturing industries in the future, although, it is possible that it will also rise low skillful workers unemployment numbers. But, the most important influence to human technological innovation will be risen and it will influence human life will be changed to be better, e.g. self drive cars, health care physician machine men, machine man cleaners etc. intelligent machine men will be manufactured to serve for our daily life. Furthermore, (AI) technological products will influence countries trading, some low technological development countries manufacturing businessmen can choose to buy any (AI) products to raise whose productivity and efficiency and reducing cost to achieve economic cost saving result. Also, GDP of trading growth income will increase to the (AI) products sale countries. Hence, it will be beneficial to economic development to both developed and developing countries both in the future as well as (AI) scientists time and money spending will be valued to continue to invest (AI) technology development for human life and economy benefits for long term.

In conclusion (AI) technology will raise macro economy growth and it can create many (AI) jobs , but it also raise the low level technological worker unemployment change. In the future, (AI) technology can be applied to digital technology to attempt to invent any new undiscovered (AI) and digital technology. So, it needs any scientists to continue to research how digital and (AI) technology can be mixed to satisfy human's future undiscovered needs.

Reference

A. Castano et. al. " Automatic detection of dust devils and clouds at Mars" Machine vision and applications, Oct. 2008, vol. 19, no 5-6, pp. 467-482.

Accenture, " Why artificial intelligence is the future of growth"(2017) <http://www.accenture.com/us-en/insight-a   rtificial-intelligence-future-growth>.

D. Schedidt , Unmanned Air Vehicle Command And Control, Handbook Of Unmanned Air Vehicles, Springer-Verlag, 2014. Facebook (AI) Research Available at https://research.facebook.com/ai, research at google, machine intelligence available at

http://research.google.com/pubs/machineintellige nce.html; micro soft research-machine learning and artificial intelligence available at http://research.microsoft.com/en-us/research-   areas/machine-learning-ai.aspx.

International Federation Of Robotics, 2016. IFR press release world robotics report. IFR, org . 29 Sept. Accessed Feb. 01, 2017. http://www.ifr.org/news/ifr-press-release/world-robitics   report -2016-8321.

K, Fedra , "GIS and environmental modelling" in environmental modelling with GIS, edited by M.F. Goodchild.B.O. Parks and L.T. Steyaert, Oxford University press, pp. 35-50, 1994.

Keynes, J.M. (1933). Economic possibilities for our grandchildren (1930). Essays in persuasion, pp.358-73.

Mckinsey & Company (2013, May). Disruptive technologies: Advices that will transform life, business and the global economy , USA.

Ministry of economy, trade and industry, Japan, 2015, Japan's robot strategy. Ministry of economy, trade and industry.

Ray Kurzweil , The age of spiritual machines (1999) is cited numerously through this chapter: Kurzweilai.net http://www.kurzweilai.net

Rich, Elaine & Knight, Kevin, Artificial Intelligence Second Edition, 1991, New York; Mc-Graw-Hill.

CHAPTER II

Can Artificial intelligence apply to digital-Transformation on jobs to raise productivity growth

Future, digital transformative technologies will how impact on economies and societies as well as how (AI) utilization of vast amounts of data to be applied to digital transformative technology. I believe that when (AI) is applied to digital transformative technology which will bring positive impacts on productivity for many firms, but it has not yet translated into stronger productivity growth at the economy –wide level. Larger impacts could result from digital technologies to all firms, notably to small and medium sized enterprises.

However, firms expected that (AI) technology and digital transformative technology can help them to raise productivity , which need have greater investments in critical complementary assets, such as firm-level skills, organizational change and process innovation as well as support for future structural change to enable the growth of new business models and digitally-intensive businesses. However, the (AI) technology is applied to digital transformative technological changes creates significant uncertainty about their future directions and impacts. Indeed, predictions about technological timelines are often inaccurate and over estimate of their short-time impacts is common.

How to achieve (AI) and the internet of things (IOT) and black chain technologies to raise productivities? It depends on large data sets and a range od digital technologies. Strong potential to improve the design implementation and evaluation of organizational policies (strategies of any firms expect to apply (AI) and internet technology combination to raise productivities.

Nowadays, global societies and private organizational firms considerate human centric (AI) needs for societies, and for further information sharing need, deepen the understanding of the potential effects of (AI) technologies on society and economies, ethics, privacy. Job creation issues. Instead of (AI) is constrained to the digital world, with significant activity to influence

, such as transport and machinery industry aspects, future (AI) technology can also be applied to service industry, such as healthcare and finance, education and training system in order to raise young people and adults right skills performance and productive efficiencies in an (AI)-enabled environment.

Hence, (AI) transformative and digital technological combination can impact those aspects to influence productivities. On gender influence aspect, Gender is particularly important in ensuring technological transformation of production change working environment. Female and male workers need to learn how to apply (AI) and digital transformative technology to work in offices or factories to strengthen their position in the labor market and in driving the digital transformation in order to achieve the aim of raising productivities. On skills safeguard against the risk of automation influence aspect, fewer than 5% of worker with a tertiary degree are at a high risk of losing their job, due to automation compared to 40% of workers with a lower secondary degree.

In future (AI) and digital technological working environment , workers needed to be equipped with a wide set of skills to be equipped with a wide set of skills as well as non-cognitive and social skills (notably information and communication technology (ICT) skills, science, technology, engineering ad mathematics (STEM) skills, and self-organization skills). Future, (AI) and digital technologies can potentially also promote social inclusion by creating education, offer-new opportunities for skills development, enhance access to healthcare industry or improve access to free and low-cost information, knowledge, and data to help organizations to improve service performance or raise productivity.

How (AI) and digital technological working environment influence job changed for employees. When, it is uncertainty about the speed of changes, it is clear that the types of jobs that are being created are not the same as those that are being lost. Moreover, the workers are affected by job loss in declining activities may not be those benefitting from the new job opportunities in any organizations. The middle –skilled jobs declining and low and high skilled jobs growing. Low –skilled workers are mostly likely to bear the costs of digital transformation, but are currently the least likely to receive training. So, the employers need to apply (AI) and digital technology to raise productivities which will influence some low-skilled workers will lose jobs, unless they can learn how to apply this new (AI) and digital technology to assist them to work in any working environments.

Better understanding the likely scope of the digital transformation and (AI) technology combination is needed to any organizations including: the growth of the big economy, or the impacts on productivity , the growing role of data, including in traditional trade is a particularly important area where sound data , i.e. data on data flow that is lacking . Although, there are still large difference in digital intensity, every firm in every sector in the economy is now being affected by the digital transformation, expanding its scope and its potential benefits. All organizations need to learn how to apply digital technology to assist whose workers to work efficiently in factories or offices in beginning. When they can learn how to apply digital technology to work. Then, they can learn how to apply (AI) technology and digital technology together to work together in order to achieve raising productivities or improve performance aims. For example, data combined with (AI) and digital technological innovation is online activity and networked things generate " big data" which feed machine learning that enables (AI), to lead to advances in intelligent machines (robotics, automated vehicles) as well as new techniques in science which can be further innovation. The growth of the volume, variety data and the ability to analyze and use it is a significant departure from the past and it causes new factor of production that argues traditional capital and labor, but unique properties of its own to be applied to office or factory manufacturing work environment in order to achieve the raising of productivity or improve performance in possible.

Why does (AI) and digital transformative combination technologies raise productivity growth or improve service performance? From 1995 to 2004 year, US experienced an acceleration in productivity growth, largely reflecting gains associated with the diffusion of ICT technologies. From the early to mid-2000 year onward, productivity growth has slowed down. The potential impacts of the ongoing digital transformation on productivity also need to consider in the context of this long term slowdown. When, the precise reasons for today's productivity remain difficult to a number of factors are likely to contribute as below factors:

The first factor that has limited the impacts of digital transformation is the state of diffusion of digital technologies across the economy. When, many firms now have across to broadband networks, the use of more advanced digital tools and application with firms still differs greatly across countries. Moreover, these are important differences between rapid technological change, advanced technologies are initially only adopted by some leading firms and then only later diffuse to all firms as the technologies because more established new business models grow, such as applying digital and (AI) technological combine method to raise productivity growth is caused and costs fall.

Consequently, these is large demand between what can be automated from a technical point of view and what may already be implemented by frontier firms and what is actually being achieve to raise productivity growth aim. So, (AI) and digital transformative technology influence future raising productivity growth or improving service aim achievement for many manufacturing and service industry demand.

The second factor indicator that the available evidence suggests that the wide-spread benefits of digitalization productivity are not enough. Firms expect to help strengthen investment (in tangible and intangible assets), e.g. (AI) technology. The same time, there are now starting to experience labor shortages, e.g. in certain technical occupations, such as data scientists. Due to the technological change is fast and growing demand for productivity growth has been increasing. SO, it will influence future (AI) robotic learning system and digital technological combination to be applied to manufacturing and service industries' needs to be raised. Due to many firms expect to find methods to raise productivity growth in order to reduce production costs.

However, (AI) and digital technological development can cause multiple forms of disruption, from shifts in demand for workforce skills to changes in market structure, the need for new business models, new patterns of trade and investment. The (AI) and digital potentially transformative technologies can create new inventions, e.g. from quantum computing and advanced energy storage to new forms of 3D printing, big data analytics and neuro-technologies. These new product creative industries must lead the new product manufacturers to expect to learn how to apply (AI) and digital technology to raise productivity growth when their manufacturing processes.

IN fact, (AI) is the ability of learning machine and system to acquire and apply knowledge and carry out intelligent behavior. Early efforts to develop (AI) centered on defining rules that software could use to perform a tack, such systems would work in speech recognition, (AI) skill. Increase in computational power, new statistical methods and advances in big data, have brought major breakthroughs to the field of (AI), especially in " vertical " (AI) like automated vehicles as opposed to " general". (AI) with machine learning algorithms that identify complex patterns in large data sets. Software applications can perform tasks and simultaneously learn how to improve productive performance. Hence, (AI) can be combined to digital world to work together with advanced in electrical engineering, it has robots to perform cognitive task in the physical world. (AI) will enable robots to adapt to new working environments with no reprogramming. Also, (AI) enabled robots will become increasingly central to logistics and manufacturing, complementing and sometimes displacing human labor in many production processes.

Future (AI) will also be developed to apply to service industry, e.g. healthcare, entertainment, marketing and finance industries. Even, future (AI) that recognizes human facial expressions and emotions could help to deliver some public services and possibly educational services. Future an essential factor achieve benefits of (AI) is the provision of reliable energy and communication networks, including for the IOT. Therefore, laws and legal frameworks may need to be considered before many of the benefits of (AI) can be bad in fields, such as transportation and healthcare industries. All above of these industries will need (AI) technology and digital technologies combination to help future manufacturing or service industries both to raise their productivity growth or improve service performance in order to reduce cost or provide more service satisfactory feeling to clients in their manufacturing processes or service processes in any manufacturing or service environments.

1.1 Apply (AI) technology to raise U.S. steel, aluminum, cooper mineral productivity growth

Future (AI) technologic robotic machines can learn how to apply 3D printer to manufacture any size and material of copied steel, aluminum , copper mineral products to be better quality in efficient productivity speed and growth. Global production of aluminum and cooper and steel mineral materials trends for global manufacturing industry is continue increasing needs to use steel, cooper, aluminum minerals to manufacture any products, e.g. car, boats, ships, furnitures, machines, buildings etc. products. However, global any products for above these mineral materials manufacturers will select the most reasonable price and the best quality of any one these minerls to select to manufacture any products which need these mineral materials or component to produce. Hence, global mineral material (component) suppliers will trend to raise these any one of minerals to produce high quality products, long term durable, reasonable price sale demand to sell to consumers.

I shall give opinions to explain that how U.S. steel, aluminum, copper mineral component suppliers need to implement what kinds of sale strategy in order to attract global steel, aluminum, copper, mineral component consumers to select to buy their steel, aluminum, cooper moneral components more easily.

Firstly, I shall discuss iron or steel sector, since the iron and steel contributes considerably to industrial Co2 emission, it is important to identify the factors driving steel demand. Two major factors will determine future CO_2 emissions in the steel sector. The first is technological progress which could lead to more efficient production technologies. However, coal which is the main source of CO_2 emissions do not only serve as a fuel in the melting process and for casting and rolling the steel. Furthermore needed for the reduction of iron ore, which makes it difficult to trim down its use beyond a certain level, even if substantial progress has been made in corrective direction. So, advanced economies, such as developed country, U.S. any steel manufacturers can attempt to use coke to manufacturer steel more efficiently. Thus, technological process in steel making is one important factor which will drive the steel manufacture and sale industry's future CO_2 emissions. The other majoe factor driving CO_2 emissions from the steel sector is future global steel demand.

In past history , in the mid-1960 year, the industry reconstruction period, which led to an increase in steel demand and production. In this period, the advanced economies were the main drivers of global steel demand. So, new production techniques are needs to global steel manufacturers. Then 1990 year, the global steel demand began to grow when many products which need steel mineral component to manufacture. In fact, steel consumption demand growth depends on two factors as below:

The first considers the industry sector and its structure , it means whether how many products need steel mineral to be supplied to manufacturer. The second considers the country's income of its population and its demand for steel manufacturing products. Hence, any U.S. steel manufacturers need to consider what kinds of unique industries which are developing in the country in order to predict the country's steel demand more accurately. For example, China's car manufacturing industry needs many steel to manufacture cars. Hence, U.S. steel manufactuers can research what steel quality, shape, price are the most attraction to sell to China car manufacturers. So, as above explanation, high technological steel manufacturing method will be one important factor to influence future U.S. steel manufacturing industry export market in success. Due to other countries which have some steel sells and some steel manufacturers who can have high technology to manufacture steel , e.g. Germany is one successful steel manufacturing country because its steel manufacturing skill had reached mature stage. Hence, U.S. needs have advanced steel manufacturing technology to raise its stel quality to win its competitors.

Hence, nowadays, global steel manufacturing industry is increasing competition. Due to the relationship between steel use and per-capita income is close. Steel consumers (steel using product manufacturers) consider to measure of technological process how the steel manufactuers apply high technology to manufacture steel products. So, high technological steel manufacturing method will be one important factor to influence steel consumers (steel using product manufacturers, e.g. car manufacturer) to select to buy their steel products in nowadays global steel manufacturing industry. Hence, U.S. steel manufacturing factories need high technological equipment to help them to manufacture the best quality, the most long durable time steel products in order to attract global steel useful steel product manufacturers to select to buy U.S.'s steel products more easily.

On income hand, it concerns global steel useful product manufacturers' income (profit), it means that U.S. steel manufacturers need to know and evaluate whether how much profit past and future global steel useful manufacturer's product consumers (business clients) that they will earn or they had earned in order to predict whether how much steel number which they will buy. It is important reason to explain why U.S. steel manufacturers need to know how much profit their business clients will earn because tehe U.S. steel manufacturers can predict whom will be their next year clients. For example, if the country one steel mineral (component) useful product manufacturing client who had loss last year. it is possible that who will reduce to buy the U.S. steel manufacturer's steel product number to prepare to manufacture how much steel number is the most accurate because its client number is less to cause loss, even it won't need any steel need to prepare to manufacture more products, e.g. cars to raise sale. Otherwise, if the country one steel mineral (component) useful product manufacturing client who had profit last year, it is possible that who will increase to buy steel products number to prepare to raise many steel mineral manufacturing need of products, e.g. cars in order to satisfy many car clients' needs in possible. So, it is possible that they (the car manufactuers) need to buy much steel to prepare to manufacture their products in this year.

Conclusion, U.S. steel manufacturers need to evaluate global steel consumers or business clients whose past and present and future financial performance in order to predict how much steel number they will need to buy as well as they also need to raise steel manufacturing equipment efficiency and performance and quality in order to raise steel productivities and qualities to keep its long time durable useful value to satisfy every steel manufacturing products' consumer' needs, e.g. cars. Hence, these two factors will be future U.S. steel manufacturing suppliers who need to concern issue in order to attract global steel mineral (component) buyers' competitive good quality of steel products needs to achieve preferable selection to their U.S. steel products to buy in global steel competitive market.

Secondly, I shall indicate U.S. aluminum, cooper, mineral manufacturing industry is similar to steel mineral manufacturing industry, but they have different competitive sale strategy. I shall explain as below:

In the future, it will be how trends in consumption and global production to select minerals of aluminium and cooper. Nowadays, to growth rate of primary production of aluminum and cooper. So, it causes threat to aluminum and cooper need for industry use, due to recycling technology can bring recycle re-use of aluminum and cooper nature to help industries to re-use any aluminum and cooper resources element to manufacture any products. So, the future trend of aluminum and cooper resources element will be reduced to global industries needs because recycling technology can bring cost benefits to let them to use recycling aluminum and cooper element. So, new aluminum and cooper resource element needs will be reduced.

Otherwise, the recycling re-used aluminum and cooper resources element has been re-used many times for the product manufacturers. Amyway, the manufacturers won't easier to select to buy new aluminum and cooper resource element. Although, the production of both primary and second recycled aluminum both have increased in fact speed. For most countries, there are no data to distinguish between production of secondary aluminum from past-consumer scrap (discarded aluminum products) and new (manufacturing) scrap. But, it seems, future trend of recycling secondary aluminum product demand is more than primary new aluminum product demand in global manufacturing industry market, such data indicated U.S. hich accounts for 50% of total world secondary aluminum product. So, it seems that secondary aluminum product (recycled) will be demanded more than primary new aluminum production. It also indicated U.S. 59% of the secondary aluminum was recovered from new scrap and 41% from post-consumer scrape. Hence, if implies future aluminum manufacturing industry consumers will select to buy secondary aluminum (recycling products) more than primary new aluminum non-used products. So, future trend in aluminum recycling product need will be reduced when nowadays aluminum resource element had been recycled to manufacture again new recycling elements many times to supply to global steel product manufacturers to re-use these nowadays recycling aluminum resource elements many times again.

I believe that future one day, when these nowadays secondary recycling aluminum resources elements had been used many times by global any product manufacturers. Then, they can be recycled to manufacture these old recycling aluminum resource element again. The effect will be that they can not be recycled to manufacture again because they had been recycled to manufactured many times. Their quality will be worst to compare primary (new) aluminum resource element to let global product manufacturers to use them to manufacture high quality of products to sell. So, I predict future primary new aluminum or cooper need will be increased because the second recycling aluminum or cooper resource element had been recycled to used to manufacture new products by different manufacturers many times. So, future the primary (new) aluminum or coooper need will be increased an dprice can also be influenced to be raised. Thus, I recommend that U.S. aluminum or cooper industrial manufacturing resource element manufacturers ought need to prepare how to seek new natural resource to manufacture primary (new) aluminum or cooper products and they ought not only concentrate on gathering reused aluminum or cooper to manufacture them again. Because , future global aluminum or cooper product consumers will prefer select to buy primary (new) aluminum or cooper more thn secondary recycling aluminum or cooper to help them to do any products to sell. So, future new (primary) aluminum or cooper product will be more proper to compare secondary recycling aluminum or cooper to seel in global industrial manufacturing market.

CHAPTER III

Can robots raise productive efficiency to raise logistic transportation speed

Can (AI) raise productive efficiency to logistic industrial sector? Technological progress in the fields of big data, algorithmic development, connectivity , cloud computing have made the performances, accessibility and costs of (AI) more favorable. Logistics is beginning to become an (AI)-driven industry, but it has also encountered challenges to overcome and opportunities to exploit. As in other industries, (AI) will extend human efficiency in terms of reach quality and speed by eliminating routine work. This will allow logistic workforces to focus in more meaningful and impactful work.

How can (AI) raise productive growth efficiency or fast manufacturing speed to logistic industry? (AI) can be defined as human intelligence exhibited by machines, syustems that approximate, replicate, automate and eventually improve on human thinking . It owns the ability to perceive , understand, learn , problem solve and reason. Whereas, (AI) is a system or device intended to amount with intelligence, machine learning is a more specific to taken in formation, usually within a specific domain, and learn from what they have been given. These learning systems draw on the ability to evaluate and categorize received data and then draw inferences from this. The output of this process is an insight decision or conclusion.

(AI) technology consists of sensing, components, processing components and learning components. SO, (IA) has this analytical process: (AI) can have deep learning ability to improve to process and understand unstructured data, e.gf. text, image, sound , then data gathered continuously from the environment, sensors and online behavior and data is aggregated. Next, machine learning framework begins to process data, patterns and trends are revealed, generated insight. Finally, the (AI) learning system takes different actions to drive value. New action is used as input to improve self-learning of system. IT is any (AI)'s full learning cycle in (AI) analytical process.

How can (AI) apply its supervised learning skills to raise productive efficiency to logistic industry? The processing and learning components and training techniques to (AI) includes" Once an (AI) system has collected data from sensing, it processes this information by applying a learning framework to generate insight from the data. IN addition to the similarities that exist between human intelligence and (AI) , strong parallels have also been observed between how humans and (AI) learning systems.

In the future, (AI) can be such a supervised learning machine man to supervise logistic workers and control and manage them how to deliver goods in warehouses more efficient. Even, they can replace human logistic workers to do their logistic tasks in warehouses. What is (AI) supervised learning system mean : It is learning that takes place when an (AI) –enabled system is directly informed by humans. I shall explain it as doctor case, A doctor who evaluates x-ray images to detect cancer risk, he/she can feed whose expert input images into an (AI) learning system to facilities supervised learning or when the (AI) learning system sorts through x-ray images for a doctor to review and approve in an effort to help improve the learning of the (AI) learning system. So, it seems that (AI) learning system can be applied to do any supervising tasks. When, (AI) robotic machines are applied to logistic warehouse environment, it can be one artificial intelligent supervisor to check any products whether are delivered to the exact locations or shelfs as well as the number of products whether it is accurate to be prepared to delivery to the outsider accurate destinations before all goods are already sent out from the warehouses. For example, Amazon publish company paper book buyers need to buy paper books , when they pay visa payment and every reader choose the right topic book from its website, when they choose to buy the topic of paper book, then Amazon publish will send the reader 's the topic book choice to its warehouse. When the logistic worker know what the topic of the paper book is sold, then the (AI) learning system will record the topic of the book and the country address of the paper book buyer to already to print the topic of paper book and send to the book buyer's address. Due to , there are many different countries paper book buyers who had chosen the different topic books to buy from amazon publish website. For example, if there are five hundred different countries book buyers who had paid visa to buy different topic books from Amazon publish website in the same day. Then , Amazon publish needs to deliver these five hundred different countries paper book buyers overseas address and the warehouse workers need to print all these five hundred different topic paper books in the same time in order to deliver all these five hundred paper books to their overseas home within two days. If Amazon publish has none of (AI) learning system to help it to record this five hundred different topic paper book buyers' overseas correct addresses and the accurate topic of every book. Then , I believe that Amazon publish has no more confidence to print the accurate different paper book right topic number and record all the different countries paper book buyers' overseas home addresses and names in order to print and deliver to them from warehouse within two days. SO, (AI) learning system can help this electronic publishing firm to record all these five hundred different countries paper book buyers' addresses and every paper book topic in its centered logistic system efficiently and effectively. Amazon publish can reduce some warehouse workers number , due to it has (AI) learning system to help it to record all paper book buyer's address and name and book topic clearly. Even, (AI) robotic machine men can help it to deliver any book to the accurate shelf location in order to delivery the right topic of every book to post to the right country's book buyer's address before all these five hundred different topic books are already posted to their overseas addresses by air planes. SO, (AI) learning system and robotics can help this publisher to manage and supervise all warehouse workers how to put these five hundred paper books to the different shelves locations more accurate in this day in warehouse. If it lacks(AI) learning system and robotic warehouse machine man to assist its warehouse workers to work in warehouse. It will increase the risk to post the wrong topic book to the wrong book buyer's address.

However, in logistic industry (AI) learning system applying key challenge facing the progress of (AI) is that logistic industry users do not trust it, because they still feel (AI) learning system can't supervise workers to deliver and distribute any products to achieve 100% accuracy in warehouses confidently. So I recommend that , the returns on (AI) investments are already improving in logistic industry and the growth in customer –facing commercial areas clearly indicates the use of (AI) learning systems and robotics in industrial sectors, such as logistic is quickly approaching. Furthermore, future many logistic companies depend on networks both physical and increasingly digital, which must function to bring these benefits, such as high products volumes and accurate numbers delivery, learn asset allocation, low margins and time-sensitive deadlines. SO, (AI) learning system and robotic machine men can offer logistic companies the ability to optimize network to degrees of efficiency and accurate number of different kinds of product deliveries, such as Amazon publish warehouse different topic printed books are delivered to overseas readers case. (AI) can also help the logistic industry to definite warehouse delivery behaviors and practices, taking operations from reactive to proactive , planning from forecast to prediction ,process from manual to autonomous, and services from standardized to personalized, warehouse delivery needs . For IBM computer products warehouse delivery case example, (AI) learning system can apply network to help IBM computer manufacturing workers to grow productivity and effectiveness of individual knowledge workers. They can be IBM manufacturing workers' assistants to assist them to manufacture any kinds of computer products in warehouse more efficiently. It can bring reducing time spending to manufacturers and (AI) robotic machine manufacturers both manufacture every computers' parts or components together in IBM warehouses. It will bring the benefits include: reducing manufacturing spending time, high productivity growth, high efficiency, avoiding manufacturing errors occurrence in IBM computer every manufacturing process.

The use of (AI) engineering and manufacturing signals a departure from the purely digital world. It can now shape the physical world around us. The manufacturing conglomerate general electric is ways to deliver power, energy and air travel. Part of the answer may be to use (AI) to inform, the production requirements and manage the continuous operation of heavy machinery to supervise products distribution, supply chain into one intelligent system in logistic warehouses. The system is connected to an intelligent order management system. Once the problem is understood and the required parts are identifies from the images , the correct parts order can be placed automatically . Finally, if specialist intervention is needed, the smart manufacturing platform can check the technician's schedule and suggest the best times for maintenance in warehouses. So, A(I) learning system can be also applied to supervise and manage warehouse works in warehouses.

Why can (AI) learning system raise productivity growth in logistic industry warehouses? (AI) learning system can be value add chain by automating existing business processes, uncovering new chain add value from data and augmenting logistic management decisions and actions . The ability to analyze levels of data that are beyond human comprehension allows logistic businesses to personalize, fast speed logistic experiences, customize products and logistic deliver services and identify productivity growth opportunities with a speed and precision that has never been positive before.

Hence, future (AI) learning system may be applied to those logistic industries , such as below:

On accurate demand forecasting beneficial aspect, in retail industry improved 1 to 2 % logistic speed to transport , improvement using machine learning to anticipate fruit and vegetable sales, 20% stock reduction using deep learning to predict e-commerce purchases, fewer product returns per year; in electric utilities industry, it can achieve objective to cut 10% in natural electricity usage by using deep learning to predict power demand and supply; on higher productivity and maintenance and repairs aspect, in retail industry , (AI) learning system has 30% reduction of stocking time using autonomous vehicles in warehouses; in electric utilities industry, (AI) learning system has 20% energy production increase using machine learning and smart sensors to optimize assets' yield as well as 10 to 20% improvement by using machine learning to enhance predictive maintenance , automate fault prediction and increase capital productivity; in manufacturing industry, (AI) learning system has 30% increase of machines delivery time using machine learning to determine timing of products' transfer and 3 to 5% production yield can be improved.

In conclusion, future (AI) learning system can enable massive productivity gains for logistic industry automating their process. Logistic industry can combine with the industrial internet of things, achieve learning can predict anomalies and sensor data, image videos and audio data and therefore reduce losses in warehouses. Moreover, manufacturers for instance are using machine learning and other (AI) techniques to better predict failure and thus to reduce maintenance costs in warehouses.

2.1 Apply (AI) technology to improve fruit and vegetable soft drink logistic transportation speed in efficient way in warehouse

Future (AI) robotic machines can be applied to help logistic workers to deliver the accurate number and weight and the right different kinds of fruit and vegetable to different locations in efficient way in warehouses. State of the plate (2015) indicated that the U.S. fruit and vegetable consumption market trend after a brief rise through 2005 year, US per capita fruit and vegatable consumption has declined 7% over the past five years, this has been driven primarily by decreased consumption of vegetables (-7%) and fruit juice (-14%). If fruit juice is excluded from the overall furit total. However, these is only a 2% decrease in fruit consumption over the past 5 year. So, fruit has seen growth among certain subsets of the population, specifically children of all ages and adult ages 18 to 44 age.

Hence, it seems that fruit juice is popular to be selected to drink for chikdren and young, adult consumers in U.S. food market. Otherwise, U.S. consumers can select either to buy fresh fruit and vegetable to eat or buy fruit juice and vegetable juice to drink in U.S. fruit and vegetable health food market. However, U.S. food consumers will have possible to decrease fruit and/or vegetable soft drink consumption. The factors include ongoing interest in consuming loe-carbohydrate foods, which peaked a decade ago, and the ever-increasing competitive set of beverages available to consumers that include flavored water. So, U.S. fruit or vegetable soft drink consumers will have possible to reduce fruit or vegetable soft drink consumption because they feel flavored water beverges or fresh fruit and vegetable will be low-carbohydrate food. Otherwise, fruit and vegetables soft drink are " sugar-sweetened" beverages. It will give less health to compare fresh fruit or vegetable food.

Why is fruit or vegetable food the main food to U.S. people daily? The reasons include that : In U.S. eating habit, fruit has enjoyed gains in U.S. people traditional consumption habit t breakfast. This is likely because breakfast is a more health related meal and fruit. For example, berries and bananas have gained favor all day, probably due to their versatility for consumption and these both fruits are as a topping for cereal or yogurt or as an ingiedient to a smoothie or hot cereal.

Future global children and young and adult and old age food consumers whether they will change their eating habit to accept fruit and vegetable soft drink to replace fresh druit and vegetable food more easily. I believe that every different age fruit and vegetable food consumer targets who will have different food need. For old age fruit and vegetable food consumer target , U.S. fruit and vegetable soft drink manufacturers need to persuade old age fruit and vegetable consumers to change their fresh fruit and vegetable food eating habit for better medical conditions , it is as a category to bring stronger health benefit to persuade higher consumption rates among older consumers. Global many old age people are concerning their health and greater incidence of medical conditions.

In specially, for the consumer ages 50 or above. Their eating habits are usually to select fresh fruit and vegetable to eat. So , it is more difficult to change their eating habits to select fruit and vegetable soft drink more easily. Unless, U.S. fruit and vegetable soft drink manufacturers can find some strong points which can influence global old people feel fruit and vegetable are not meeting in terms of their health and daily lives. Other influential factors which will be possible to influence their food and fruithabit changing to select fruit and vegetable for their daily lives need, e.g. reasonable price, better taste, shopping convenience. For example, yogurt is a natural gaining for fruit or vegetable and some fruit can work well on pizza or a variety of vegetables can be included on poultry sandwiches. All of these complementary food groups are also among th fastest growing food items. They can have much competitive effort to influence global traditional fresh fruit and vegetable consumers to select to buy these kinds of complementary fruit and vegetable to eat sometimes in daily lives because they can provide fresh taste of food choice, due to their taste will have some different feeling to let global fresh fruit and vegetable consumers to fee when they are eating. Also, choice of anywhere locations to sell fruit and/or vegetable soft drink, this factor is also important. In retail, these has been a lot of focus on the perimeter of the store, but the center of the fruit and vegetable soft drink store location is important and fruit and vegetable soft drink or yougurt natural drink for fruit product or vegetables and some fruit pizza or a variety of vegetables include on sandwiches which can be sold on different countries' cities restaurants or food retail shops or pizza retail stores which can be selected to locate to any country's central cities in order to attract travellers or working people to find these restaurants conveniently to buy different kinds of manual manufacturing of fruit and/or vegetable taste of soft drink or food restaurants to drink or eat for breakfast, lunch or dinner.

In conclusion, the future global future fruit and vegetable soft drink consumption influential factors will include taste, retail locaion choice, drink or food element manufacturing factor in order to attract global fresh fruit or fresh vegetable food consumers' consideration If U.S. fruit and vegetable soft drink food manufacturers expect to change global fruit and vegetable food consumers' traditional eating habits easily. They must have good sale plans for how to maufacture attractive taste, how to select suitable locations to sell and how to charge the price to let global different fruit and vegetable food consumers to feel their fruit and vegetable soft drink products are more reasonable price to compare traditional fresh fruit and vegetable food. However, fruit and vegetable will have possible to be not fresh when they are saved long time in any stores or farms location. Otherwise, fruit and vegetable soft drink will have long time to save to ice box to wait to drink. So, it is maunal manufacturing of fruit and vegetable soft drink food product's stronger point to compete to natural fruit and vegetable food.

2.2 Applying (AI) technology to improve global daily food logistic transporation speed in warehouses

Future (AI) robotic machines can assist warehouse workers to deliver the accurate number and right different kinds of daily drinks, e.g. milk, orange juice, apply juice, soft drinks, milk, cheese, ice-cream etc. different kinds of soft drinks and food to different right loacations in efficient way and the fast transportation speed in warehouses. The research and insights committee indicated that it discovered U.S. daily food industry had no loger significant increases in gross dometic product and population expansion to drive domestic growth. So, it brings this challenge for U.S. daily food product manufacturers' cost savings / gains driven and production efficiencies will be possible caused to U.S. daily food product caused to U.S. daily food product manufacturers in domestic market. So, they ought consider how to expand overseas daily food product market to attempt to increase more different kinds of daily products to different countries. I shall recommend some solutions as below:

U.S. daily food product manufacturers ought plan future five to ten year opportunities to drive the growth of daily / daily -based food products to overseas different countried. For example, Hong Kong, China, Japan Asia countries have many people who like to buy U.S. daily food to eat or drink, e.g. milk, cheese, ice-cream. So, they need have good identification of macro trends and a greater understanding of data-based key elements (e.g. the country's demographic shifts, prediction of the country has how many people who like to eat or drink any kinds of daily food, e.g. Japan's one city Tokyo has how many people who like to eat or drink any kinds of U.S. daily food ; finding every country's people whose food / eating behaviors, e.g. in what suitation which will influence Japanese have desire to buy daily food, such as the consumption group , e.g. prediction of young or old age Japanese number will like to eat or drink U.S. daily food in what time of one day for the old or young age Japaneses' eating habit, e.g. morning time, luch time or dinner time. So, the U.S. daily food manufactuers can follow the suitable time to prepare sell the accurate number to Japan. For example, if they predict there are 500,000 about Japanese young and old age people who like to buy U.S. daily food to eat or drink after dinner time in Tokyo city every week. Then, they can export enough different kinds of daily food number to Tokyo every week ; retail channel shift , e.g. supermarket ot small retil store ; food service promotion perspective , .e.g. newspaper or magazone or radio daily food service promotion channel choice to let the country people to know what kinds of U.S. daily food can be sole to the country. Then, these methods can help any U.S. daily food manufacturers have potential to predict the accurate consumption number to every coutries and U.S. itself to raise their daily food export or local sale number.

These methods aim to investigate whether what kinds of daily food products sale to the country's people who will be accepted to buy to eat or drink more. For example, how many Japanese are living in the city , e.g. Tokyo , who like to buy milk, daily beverages, cheeses, yogurt, frozen daily and daily is as an ingredient or a component food to eat or drink. Thus, market research can help the U.S. daily food manufacturers to attempt to predict every export country's different cities daily food product buyer number and predict what kinds of daily food will be popular to choose to eat or drink for the country's different cities' peoples' eating culture or habit. So, U.S. daily food manufacturers need have a leading global strategic planning to predict future how consumer insights and trends will how and why and when change in order to make more accurate daily food customer behavioral predictive analysis to satisfy the country's daily food product consumer need and making the more accurate suitable population daily food sale distribution for different kinds of daily food products to the country.

The daily food market research strategiss plan will be marked by increasing rates of change driven by key macro forces as below:

Firstly, U.S. daily food manufacturers need to evaluate uncertainty over policies, economy, supply and different kinds of daily food prices will be possible to increase traditional middle income Americans and global daily food consumer number. It depends on their brands whether are familiar to their daily food consumers because U.S. daily food industry will need to evaluate how global market environment economic changes and daily food product supply is predicted to the different kinds of sale number and global daily food product consumer's demand in order to measure the most accurate sale price to different kinds of daily food to let global daily food consumers to feel the brand of daily food suppliers' sale prices are more reasonable in order to raise its consumer number and define the both low-end (social reasonable acceptance of premium sale price strategy) in global competitive daily food market.

Secondly, U.S, daily food manufacturers need to innovate or improve their manufacturing method to raise different kinds of daily food products' qualities, improving daily food product formulation , e.g. taste, health food elements, attractive daily food and consumer beneficial package and advertising doctors' medical health confirmation message offerings to let global daily food consumers to know. Due to nowadays, global (including U.S.) daily food product consumer number will be increasingly diverse and more globally aware (aging population, growing and extending to a more diverse youth demographic daily food product consumer trend). The changing face and resultant health conditions of global daily food product consumers will require daily food as well as brands of different kinds of daily health food products' food health quality will be needed to raise in order to satisfy their health food needs.

Finally, smart shopping technology will be increasing demand to U.S. different brands of daily food manufacturers. Global health daily food consumers will choose to buy any kinds of daily food from digital technology, i.e. online shopping is one kind of fast long distance distance point of purchase decision making capabilities. Also, smart shopping technology will alter and raise global daily food product consumers' health food expectations of retail to more of an experience. So, how to select sale channels to buy the brand's daily health food which will be one important factor to influence every brand of daily food product manufacturer in success because global daily food product consumers had been influenced by internet onlye shopping channel. For example, U.S. some daily food consumer who are living far away from cities, if their home locations has no any supermarkets, and they need to drive long time to arrive the locations where have supermarkets. Then, they need to choose to buy any kinds of daily food products from internet because daily food product price is cheap and purchase number is less. So, they will compare the journey of their gas spending needed to drive their cars and driving time from homes to supermarkets as well as internet online shopping channel.

Usually, if U.S. daily food product consumers will prefer to choose to buy these kinds of daily food from internet channel when they need to drive cars to go o supermarkets. The reasons is because that they can earn more economic benefits of less time and less cost from internet online shopping channel to compare driving cars to go to supermarkets channel to buy the only daily food product every time. For example, their daily food today sale product include, yogurt, cheese, fozen food etc. these kinds of daily food products which are the most popular to buy from internet online channel for the living far away supermarkets to satisfy lower order convenience needs for internet online shopping channel. This reason is supported on behavioral economic theory to explain why internet online shopping channel is more acceptance to the living far away from supermarkets.

In conclusion, any brands of U.S. daily food product manufacturers ought consider these above any strategies in order to raise their competitive effort in global daily food product market in success more easily. When they apply (AI) learning system technology to improve their transportation speed efficiently.

2.3 Applying (AI) technology improve U.S. future alcohol, wine drink products logistic transportation speed in warehouses

Future (AI) robotic mahcines can assist warehouse workers to transport the accurate number of right alcohol, wine drink products to different locations in efficient speed in warehouses.Nowadays, some economists predicted U.S. to be the largest wine, alcohol the largest drinking consumer. What are the factors cause U.S. has effort to be grown demand in global wine or alcohol industry. I shall follow the global economic changing factors to estimate how and why global wine consumers' behaviors are influenced to choose to buy U.S. wine or alcohol by global economic changing factor influences.

One reason is found evidence which is based on winr or alcohol quantify determinants of global wine consumption influence. It seems that U.S. every year wine or alcohol manufacturing number will influence global wine or global consumers why to choose U.S. wine or alcohol to drink. I shall explain why economic factor will influence U.S. wine supply number. For example, when the year, it has oversupply of grapes to import to U.S. for wine manufacturers to manufacture and kinds of wine drinking products, which made possible the introduction of extreme value wines in U.S. country.

When the global economic environment is good, many people has jobs to work. Then, it will cause many people consider to choose to buy the better quality of different kinds of wine to drink, due to global many people have extra money to save. They have effort to spend to drink at lest one bottle better quality of wine to drink. Thus, the global wine drinker number will increse. With the rise in per capita income in U.S. itself country and other countries as well as the year oversupply of grapes import number can be supplies to let U.S. any wine manufacturers to manufacture different kinds of better quality wine in order to sell to overseas and U.S. domestic wine drinkers. Thus, in the year, the demand for higher qiality food and beverages , e.g. wine is expected to rise , due to the year economic environment is good and U.S. oversupply number of grape to prepare to manufacture different kinds of better quality wine in order to satisfy global high quality wine drinkers' taste needs.

Hence, it proves that global economic environment changing factor and U.S. better quality of wine supply factor will influence U.S. wine drinker number. If the year economic environment is bad, global many people lose jobs and the farming growth environment is poor, it has not good climate to grow many grapes to rise their number for U.S. wine manufacturers to manufacture any kinds of wine products. Then, U.S. wine supply number and global better quality of wine drinker number both will decrease. Thus, global economic environment and U.S. better quality of wine drinkers' demand will have direct or indirect relationship to influence U.S. wine sale number.

Other U.S. wine export number successful factor considers U.S. wine manufacturers ought consider different countries' wine drinkers' taste , reasonable sale price demand and their drinking wine culture (drinking habit). Historically, U.S. wineries adopter either of three methods to sell any kinds of wines drinking product. They include lifestyle, product or production. I shall explain as below;

Firstly, lifestyle means tht every country's wine consumers will have themselves wine drinking culture or habit to choose which kinds of wine or alcohol drinking product to drink. So, if any U.S. wine drink product manufacturers can know the country's wine consumers' preferable wine product choice.

Then, they can evaluate whether which kinds of wine product to decide to sell to the country more accurate and easily, product of wine. It means that they can know how to produce high quality wine products, e.g. using how much grapes or lemons or oranges or apples etc. fruit element and sugar and how to keep the suitable temperature to save every bottle of wine in wine stores in whole wine manufacturing procedure efficiently in order to manufacture the best taste of different kinds of fruit wine to sell to the different countries' target consumers to sell. Because different countries' wine consumers who have different taste preferable needs and wine qualities and drinking culture (habit) needs. So, they need to gather data concerns different countries' wine drinking consumers' preferable choice needs in order to choose the best suitable kinds of wine taste to sell to the country prope to drink.

Finally, it is production cost aspect, it concerns how much costs of every kind wine to manufacture every kind of wine products. It is very important to influence every U.S. wine suppliers' consumer number because if it's production cost, e.g. finished wine product lorry transportation cost in U.S. domestic places between the wine manufactuer's factory and wine stores or fruit transportation farming places and its wine manufacturer's factory which transportat cost is high as well as overseas air plane fruit transportation cost to be delivered the wine manufacturer's factory or the U.S. finished wine products are needed to transport to overseas wine market to sell to different countries' air plane freight cost which is high, then these transportation cost will influence the U.S. wine seller's sale price to be raised if it needs often to deliver any wine finished products to overseas or domestic win both markets. Then, the U.S. wine manufacturers' high delivery behavioral cost will impact to global wine consumers' desires to be fallen down because they will feel its sale price is not too reasonable high to reduce their wine consumption desires.

In conclusion, these three aspects of factors, which are every U.S. wine drinking product manufacturers need to consider before they achieve to do any kinds of wine businesses.

The other research considers U.S.alcohol consumption in U.S. and overseas markets. Alcohol is different to wine because some people feel alcohol, e.g. beer . It can hurt human's health, when the alcohol drinker often drinks beer. Otherwise, wine is health drinking product to global drinking consumers' feeling usually. So, U.S. alcohol manufacturers' consumers target will be limited to sell to the people who do not worry about any kinds of alcohol product , e.g. beer which can burt to their health. Unless, U.S. alcohol manufacturers can being good message to change the alcohol drinking consumers' attitudes to feel any alcohol products won't hurt whose health. Hence, U.S. alcohol manufacturers need have good methods to let global alcohol drinking consumers change to drink alcohol attitudes to let them to feel alcohol won't influence their health when they sometimes or often drink alcohol.

Hence, how to change their drinking alcohol habit to be accepted to drink alcohol behaviors which won't bring hurt to influence their health , this changing of drinking alcohol habit or attitude issue which will help any U.S. alcohol manufacturers to increase alcohol consumer number in long term. So, it is one valuable researching matter to any U.S. alcohol manufacturers. Moreover, it is valuable to underatand the trends and possible future patterns for alcohol consumption by beverage type given that the consumption of some alcoholic beverage types trends to have more strongly relationship with outcomes or actions that increase externality costs and negative health outcomes.

Also, U.S. alcohol manufacturers need to consider that every country's government charges how much alcohol taxes to import countries' alcohol manufactuers because any U.S. alcohol manufacturers will choose to raise higher alcohol sale price if the country government needs them to charge higher alcohol taxes to import t the country. Then, it will bring negative emotion influence to the high alcohol import tax country's alcohol consumers, due to the U.S. alcohol manufacturers charge higher sale price to their different kinds of alcohol products immediately. The sudden alcohol raising price factor will influence the high alcohol imported tax country's alcohol consumers feel any kinds of U.S. alcohol products won't be onre kind of health drinking product, due to their sale prices are raised suddenly. They will consume to drink othe kinds of U.S. drinking products, e.g. fruit juice, wine to replace U.S. alcohol drinking products. So, any U.S. similiar alcohol taste products will be the export alcohol drinking product manufacturers' competitors if the U.S. alcohol manufacturer's one alcohol imported country plans to raise 10 to 20%, even more alcohol imported tax to their alcohol products next month. Then, the imported alcohol country's alcohol consumer number will be caused to reduce more easily. Hence, any U.S. alcohol manufacturers need to consider when the import alcohol countries will raise alcohol imported tax to charge them in order to select other low alcohol imported tax or no raising imported tax countries to increase to export more alcohol products to them to replace the high tax countries alcohol imported to keep their competitive effort and build good brand to the U.S. alcohol manufacturers' image to the high alcohol imported tax countries' alcohol consumers to let them to feel the brand of U.S. alcohol manufacturer's alcohol is still valuable to select to buy to drink.

2.4 Apply (AI) technology improve US pork food logistic transportation speed in warehouse

Future , (AI) robotic machies can assist warehose workers to deliver the accurate pork food number and right weight to different locations in warehouses before they are delivered to different supermarkets or pork store sellers. Nowadays, pork ranks third in annual US meat consumption, behind beef and children averaging 51 pounds per person. US pork consumption varies by race and ethnitity. In general, US blacks race people consume 63 pounds of pork per person per year, whites race people 49 pounds and Hispanics 45 pounds. Otherwise, higher income US consumers tend to consume less pork.

Demographic data in the CSFII suggest future declines in per capita pork consumption, as increases of Hispanics and the elderly in US , who eat less port than the national average, enlarge their shared of the population. However, total US pork consumption will grow because of an expansion of the US population, e.g. US immigrants number will increase from different overseas.

In fact, although pork isn't consumed by certain populations or certain regions, it is one of the preferred meats in the world and United States. So, understanding the basic factor underlying pork consumption wil help US to supply in pork market and will able the meat industry to as well as it well the enable the industry (Economic research service, 2004).

In conclusion, US pork high income and white race consumers do not prefer to select pork to eat. it is possible due to they feel port is most common meat and purchase easily food. Hence, pork manufacturer (suppliers) ought raise pork sale quality and better taste, e.g. ungrade common pork from low meat quality and poor taste class meat to raise to high meat quality and better taste class meat to compare beef and sheep meet substitutes. Hence, building good public image to pork that is very importnt to influence US pork domestic consumption market, even overseas markets. This issue is all US pork suppliers need to consider if they expect to raise pork meat consumption effort in success in long term future.

CHAPTER IV

Applying artificial intelligence and machine learning to improve tourism service performance to satisfy travellers needs.

Future, predicting artificial intelligence (AI) and machine learning technology will be rapidly adopted for a range of application in the tourism entertainment industry. I shall explain how to apply (AI) to improve service performance for any kinds of financial service clients.

In the future, (AI) will be increased to supply to satisfy different kinds of tourism entertainment to satisfy whose needs to raise tourism service performance. The needs include: Tourism agents or airlines will use (AI) and machine learning methods to access air paper air ticket or electronic air ticket price to automate travelling client interaction. They are optimizing scarce capital will (AI) and machine learning techniques, as well as back-testing models and analyzing the tourism market impact of tourism entertainment need larger positions

Why and how (AI) and learning system can improve tourism service performance for any tourim institutions. The more efficient processing of information for example in travelling destiantion choice decisions and travelling customer interaction may contribute to a more efficient travelling destination choice system and it can help improve regulatory compliance and increase effectiveness. At the same time, network effects and scalability may give rise to third-party dependencies.

Applications of (AI) and machine learning can be variable to meet various financial institutions' needs. The uses of (AI) and machine learning will help tourism agent or airline institutions' clients to reduce personal or financial risk, e.g. data privacy, conduct risks. Also, adequate testing and training of tools with data and feedback mechanisms is important to ensure applications do what they are intended to do. So, (AI) and machine learning technology can be applied to financial industry as these aspects: customer -focused application, operation-focused uses application, trading and portfolio management application aspects.

(AI) big data is used broadly to storage and analysis of large and / or complicated data sets using a variety of techniques including (AI). The analytics often related to the amount of unstructured or sem-structured data in data sets. The technology can be applied to help any tourism agents or airline institutions to improve service performance. Machine learning may be defined a method of designing a sequence of actions to solve a problem, known as algorithms, which optimise automatically through experience and with limited or no human intervention. These techniques can be used find patterns in large amounts of data (big data analytics) from increasingly diverse and innovations sources to help any tourism or airline institutions for be supervised to learn to be improve service performance from every time the travelling client's tourism entertainmentn any countries.

Why can (AI) deep learning algorithms be applied to tourism entertainment industry to raise service performance? For encoding the concept of a car case example, It is from a series of discovering generalisable concepts, such as encoding images. So, an investor might deploy an alogorithm to gather data to predict retail store sale numbers in a particular period. An alogorithm can recognise cars to count the number of cars in a retail parking lot of from a satellite image in order to infer a likely stores, sale figure for a particular period.

As applicationing to tourism entertainment service case, natural language processing of deep learning algorithms can allow computers to read and produce written text or when combined with voice recognition to read and produce spoken language to translate different countries language to let travellers to understand that the country can provide anywhere to let overseas travellers to go to its country to choose to travel . For financial loan case example, (AI) big data technology can also help financial institutions to decide whether the firm has ability to pay back loan and interest . When it borrow loan from the financial institution. This technology will help the financial institution to gather past data to evaluate and analyze its credit rate report more accurate than manual judgement. Even, it can help the financial institutions to evaluate how much loan amount can be lent to the more accurate in order to decide its loan pay back period and load and interest calculation amount to conclude the accurate lending loan service and interest charge amount to the firm (loan borrower) more confident.

Another example , it might be to automatically apply (AI) big data technology to read sale report or estimate an unrated company's intitial credit client's financial situation in order to evaluate whether the financial loan service firm has effort to pay its loan and interest to the financial company in the particular period in possible Since cloud computing and internet technology created this new website technology can combine to (AI) deep learning algorithms.

In order to collect big amount, big data concerns the financial company's client's financial transactions in short time, e.g. big data on the scale of every single credit card transaction interconnectedness of information technology resources with cloud computing with whose big data can now be organized and analyzed. Using big data sets of this size and complexity and with the increase in cloud computing power, machine learning algorithms client's financial situation results more accurate than every financial consultant individual judgement.

In conclusion, human intelligence learning machine can replace or assist human financial consultants' some logic or complexity financial analysis tasks in any financial service organization's departments in order to reduce their workloads to achieve to improve financial service performance to their clients more satisfactory or effectively. Even future (AI) learning machine and big data and internet combination technology can bring these benefits to any financial service organizations, such as faster processor speeds, lower hardware cost, and better access to computer power via cloud computing services. If the financial service organization chose to apply (AI) machine learning technology to share financial service workers' tasks in different departments. It will bring to improve better service performance and reduce cost for the financial service organization in possible.

3.1 How to apply (AI) technology to improve service performance to satisfy US tourism consumers needs

Nowadays, tourism industry is every country's main leisure income. Every country will need have itself unique tourism features to attract travellers to go to travel easily. So, attractive unique tourism features can persuade different countrues travellers choose to go to itself country to travel more easily. I shall recommend what factors can influence global travelling consumers choose to go to US travel more easily. The travelling strategies can attempt to be implemented as below:

Firstly, US tourism leisure providers (travel agents) need to know what different countries' tourism consumers why and how to persuade them to feel US anywhere places are valuable to go to travel, what can attract them in these places, for Chinese travellers case example, what Chinese like to play when they choose to go to any one of the US domestic travelling placs. So, the US tourism leisure providers need to define the Chinese tourism consumers' tourism acts, attitude and travelling decisions regarding choosing, buying and consuming tourism products and tourism services and also its past consumer tourism reaction. Due to different countries' tourism consumers who have different tourism leisure needs, e.g. Chinese young age travellers prefer to choose to tourism package arrangement, who only like to buy air tickets and arrange their travelling journeys, e.g. they can choose where they will live and anywhere they choose to travel. So, US tourism service providers only concentrate on introducing anywhere US places valuable to let them to travel, calculating every journey transportation cost, and living and eating cost to let Chinese young tourism consumers to know. Otherwise, Chinese old age tourism consumers prefer to the US tourism service providers can arrange whole tourism journey to help them to reduce their worries about paying how much rent to live hotels, transportation costs in US anywhere journeys. Due to US is a large area country, many Chinese will feel worry about how to catch the bus, ferry, domestic air place, taxt, train , tram etc. transportation to go to any US domestic tourism places to pay the cheaper cost as well as how to find the reasonable price of hotels to live as well as how to choose the most valuable travelling places to travel and US anywhere touism places can be exciting and comfortable and enjoyable tourism leisure feeling in their whole US tourism journeys.

In special, the Chinese old age tourism consumers must consider above these challenges, they must need the US tourism leisure provider ensures to help them to arrange all their US tourism journey needs, then they will reduce worry to choose who is the best tourism leisure service provider if the US travel service provider can solve above all challenges for their US domestic journeys. So, the US doemstic tourism leisure arrangement service market competition is serious. Every US domestic tourism leisure provider needs have unique travelling leisure arrangement to attract them.

Secondly, US tourism service providers need to attempt to find different countries' tourism consumers' tourism leisure needs and how they make travelling journey decision processes because it can assist marketing manger to improve his/her own decision making process to forecast future different countries' tourism consumers' behaviors and to have a real and objective image of the country's general tourism consumer tourism leisure and tourism journey arrangement demands.

Hence, US tourism leisure service providers need to spend time to gather past different countries' tourism journeys arrangement tourism experience to develop new tourism products and services . It will include these questions for each country's travelling consumers' demands, such as below:

Who is important in the whole travelling journey arrangement decision making final tourism consumer?

What are the criteria every family or friend travelling group consumers' choice based on? e.g. travelling journey cost includes hotel, food, air ticket, leisure activities expenditure critera or how many days of the whole travelling journey criteria.

Where or when do they buy air ticket?

All these criteria will influence every tourism group consumer to make final travelling decision making to choose the US travelling servie provider or another one. Hence, when predicting travelling consumers buying processes, sometimes the travelling service provider will make false assumptions about these processes can result in an wrong assumption. Otherwise, good tourism journey arrangement product or service is not being bought. But, every time of making false assumption will raise the more accurate judgement effort to predict future every country's travelling consumers' journeys' arrangement and improve their travelling journey arrangement skill when their every time of false assumption. Hence, every US travel service provider won't need to fear fail to make false assumption. Otherwise, they need to revise every time false assumption in order to improve next time travelling jounrey arrangement service quality in order to raise their satisfactory level.

Thirdly, US travelling service providers need to understand what the factors can influence overseas travelling consumers' behavior. The factors include the personal factor, such as tourist's personality, self image, attitudes, motivations, perceptions, life style, age, family life style, profession. For example, if the travelling consultant felt the tourist, he/she likes to contact exciting things, then he/her travelling leisure will be the exciting travelling destinations, e.g. Walt Disney theme park, climing mountain sport, riding bicycles on hill sport, swimming sport, catching fast speed train transportation tool tourism journey arrangement. Otherwise, if the travelling consultant felt the tourist, he/she likes to contact quiet things, then his/her travelling leisure will be the quiet travelling destinations, e.g. walking around shopping centers, visiting book shops , walking on beaches etc. US cities or countryside walking travelling journey arrangement.

The another factor concerns the country's social culture, family, social class, reference groups. For example, Japanese social culture is common high social class to compare Chinese, Indian etc. So, their travelling demand will be higher to compare Chinese and Indian. For example, they like to eat better taste of food, when they choose to go ro anywhere to travel. So, US travellers need to arrange the better taste of food to eat. However, whether the US journey which have arrange Japan restaurant or Indian restaurant or Chinese restaurant to provide Japan food or Chinese food or India food taste to these countries travellers to eat. It is very important to influence any countries tourism consumers to choose to go to US to travel.

The other factor concerns situational factor, such as time, psychology, ambiance, social ambiance, state of mind. The country's good or bad social culture can influence travelling consumption motivation attitude. For example, when the country had good social culture to encourage the country's people to spend money to travel easily. So, this kind unconscious or conscious motivations are encouraged by the social culture to its living people. Then, its living people will be encouraged to select, organize and interpret sensory stimulation into a meaningful tourism picture of the world. So the country's good travelling leisure social culture will encourage the country's people to accept to spend money to go to anywhere for travelling leisure easily. It is one social tourism culture to encourage the country people to spend money to travel when they have holidays. So, any US tourism leisure service providers need to know what the country's social culture is in order to select the most suitable travelling destinations to attract them to travel to themselve America country more easily.

The other factor concerns age which is an effective discriminator of tourism consumer behavior. For example, young travellers have every different tourism tastes as regards travelling products or travelling trip service arrangement to compare to old travellers. Also, young age travellers tend to spend more than old age travellers. Thus, if the travelling service provider can predict what travelling needs of the old or young age traveller segments which can rise interest in tourism marketing from those tourism behavior point of view are: childhood , teenage, first youth, second youth and old age different tourism age segments' unique tourism leisure arrangement and tourism service and evaluate whether the travelling package price is the most reasonable to satisfy their different tourism age segments needs in order to evaluate the most reasonable travelling package price charge. Moreover, profession also has a great impact on tourism consumer behavior, profession young or old tourism segment and non-profession young or old tourism segment, due to their education level has high or low difference. So, its impact over an individual tourism decision is obvious difference. For example, professional young or old age travellers can have more money to spend high class expensive tourism leisure. So, tourism journey arrangement can be belonged to a medium or high class. They usually demand high rates accomodation and meal and expensive train, air plane, ferry etc. transport tools in their auxiliary services during the journey. Otherwise, non-professional young or old age travellers can not have enough money to spend high class expensive tourism leisure. So , tourism journey arrangement can be belonged to a low class. They usually demand low rates accomodation and meal and cheap tram, train , air plane, ferry etc. transportion tools in their poor services during the journey.

Thus, US tourism firms will need have interest in attracting opinion leader because their abilities to influene groups and try to convince them regarding the tourism service quality of their tourism service needs.

The final factor concerns economic factor. It is the most sensitive to environmental change and it is as a result, US tourism service providers have been very affected by the global economic situation influence.

In the past, tourism plays an important role in the European economy. Many labor were dominated by this tourism industry, due to global number of visitors has been increasing fastly in the past between ten to twenty years. Thus, the global economy is influenced to recovery, being influenced by economies from Asia and America which register continued and considerable increases.

As Europe tourism industry case,many countries implemented domestic tourism visitor number measures, delaying the economic recovery perspectives, already weak. The euro and American dollar, but the possibilities tourist from all over the world, with of special offers and low price vacations. Thus, economic factor influences dollar exchange change which will also influence global travellers choose whether they ought need choose Asia or Europe or America to travel by exchange dollar variable factor influence.

Hence, US tourism leisure service providers need to concernn global economic environment how will change in order to make solutions to avoid global travellers choose to go to Asia or Europe or America to travel, due to these countries' money exchange rate can bring beneficial to let them to spend less than choice to go to US travel. So, it implies that economic changing behavior can influence global tourism consumers to choose to go to America to travel, even their earlier tourism country is US.

In conclusion, all these factors will influence global travellers' tourism countries choices and tourism leisure activities and tourism journey arrangement choices serious. Thus, US tourism leisure providers need to consider global economy will how change and discover many different kinds of tourism leisure arrangement package in order to arrange the different kinds of the most suitable tourism leisure package to satisfy global tourism consumers' unique tourism leisure consumer segments' needs.

CHAPTER V

Can artificial intelligence raise productivity growth efficiency in industrial sector

When (AI) robotic technology is applied to any industrial sectors, instead of replacing or helping labor workers to do some simple tasks to share their workload beneficial aspect, whether it can really help them to raise productivity growth or work efficiency in any industrial working environments. Which are subindustries the most strongly affected by the automation potential of (AI)? How can managers of industrial players cooperate with (AI) and workers work efficiently in order to achieve to raise productivity growth aim?

Future (AI) technology can bring two aspects of benefits in industrial sector manufacturing operations and business processes both aspects as below:

On manufacturing operations aspect, predictive maintenance is enhanced by (AI) allows for better prediction and avoidance of machine failure by combining data from advanced internet of things (IOT) sensors and maintenance logs as well as external sources. So, asset productivity can increase of up to 20% are possible , and overall maintenance costs may be reduced up to 10%; collaborative aware robots will improve production through based on (AI) enabled human machine interaction in labor-intensive settings. Therefore, productivity increases up to 20% are feasible for certain-tasks, even when tasks are not fully automatable; yield enhanccement in manufacturing powered by (AI) will result in decreased scrap rates are testing costs by linking various across machinery groups and sub-processes, e.g. in the semi-conductor industry, the use of (AI) can lead to a reduction in yield detraction by up to 30%. Moreover, automated quality testing can be realized using (AI). By employing advanced image recognition techniques for visual inspection and fault detections productivity increases of up to 50% are possible. Specificantly, (AI) based visual inspection based on image recognition may increase defect detection rates up to 90% as compared to human inspection.

On business processes beneficial aspect, (AI) enhanced supply chain management greatly improves forecasting accuracy when increasing and optimizing stock replenishment. Reductions between 20 and 50% in forecasting errors are feasible. So, lost sales due to products not being available can be reduced by up to 65% and inventory reductions of 20% to 50% are achieved; The application of machine learning to enable high-performance R&D projects has large potential. So, research and research cost reductions of 10 to 15% and time-do-market improvements up to 10% are expected. Finally, business support function automation will ensure improvements in both process quality and efficiency. Automation rates of 30% are possible across functions. For the specific example IT service desks, automation rates of 90% are expected.

Can (AI) automatin technology innovate the future of production? Trends towards higher levels of automation causes greater speed and precision of producton as well as reduced exposure to dangerous tasks for employees. New production technologies could help overcome the stagnant productivity and make may for more valued added activity in production sector.

Exciting advances in the internet of things, artificial intelligence, advanced robotics, wearables and 3 D printint are transforming what, where and how products are designed, manufactured, assembled, distributed, consumed, service after purchase, even reused. They affect and alter all end-to-end steps of the production process and as a result, transform the products that consumers demand, the factory process and the management of global supply chains, addition to industry pecking orders and countries' access. So, future (AI) robotic technology will be applied to those production sectors. They include 80% of wearables market and almost 70% of industrial 3D printing units. Other specific industries with automotive, electronics and aerospace being early adopter in most cases to apply (AI) robotic technology to help their workers to work more efficient and to achieve productivity growth.

In fact, competitive production is demanded to reduce cost in higher manufacturing cost environmeents. (AI) robotic technology will have possible to help manufacturers to reduce cost, e.g. when the production environment occurs in the capital-intensive sectors with high transportation costs . So, if the manufacturer does not choose to apply (AI) robotic manufacturing technology to help it to assist workers to manufacture in factory. Then, it's traditional manufacturing technology will negatively impact white and blue-collar workers on the factory floor if societies do not ready their workforce for the new (AI) robotic skill sets and put in place transition mechanisms to ease negative impacts.

Future, (AI) robotic technology will bring these advantages to manufacturing industry's production process: Mapping a comprenhensive technology to impact one or more aspects of global production systems. Exercises followed to prioritize and focus analysis on deemed to have the broadest applicability across value chain elements; a foresight series was created for each production (AI) robotic technology. Capturing current technical readiness and adoption levels across (AI) robotic production processes, manufacturing industries focusing on the impact of the (AI) robotic production technologies by understanding the connections between (AI) robotic manufacturing technology and traditional non-(AI) robotic manufacturing technology and they compete in solving firm by social production process problems and by bringing the positive production method impact on the factory floor and on firms, industries, societies and individual manufacturing needs.

For example, advanced robotics can be applied to 3 D printing technological manufacturing copied product tasks from digital -physical transformation. So, (AI) robotics can replace workers to do any 3D printing tasks to copy any products. The benefits to change the factory's physical location to be small areas, high speed network, raising producers' revenues (new offering, business models) and reducing cots (selling, administrative expenses, logistic etc.) , less long term investments and capabilities to achieve 3 D printing product increasing number in efficient (AI) robotic working speed. Although , it is possible to destroy factory labor worker 3 D printing product job, but it can create new 3 D printing (AI) robotic controller working jobs to be technicians to teach (AI) robotic machines to learn how to use 3 D printer to manufacture any copied products. The most important benefit of 3D robotic machines replacing labor 3D printing labors that is the manufacturer can reduce labor 3 D printing worker number, due to the manufacturer applies (AI) robotic to assist the 3D printing workers to fo every step of manufacturing copied product tasks. So, the 3D printing (AI) robotic machine labors can replace all 3 D printing labor workers to do every step to apply 3 D printers to manufacture every copied product. Otherwis, the 3 D printing copied product manufacture will employ the (AI) robotic technicians to control and supervise and teach the (AI) robotic 3 D printing product machines to learn how to use the 3 D printers to do every step to manufacture different kinds of copied products to sell in the market. Hence, the 3 D printer copied product manufacture will reduce labors and salary when it applies 3 D printing robotic machine labors to replace labor workers to finish every printing step to manufacture different kinds of copied products in factory. for example, when the 3 D printing technicians had taught the robotic machine to learn how to apply 3 D printer to manufacture a copied vehicle's motor engine. Then, the (AI) robotic machine had learnt how to apply the 3D printer to manufacture different kinds of copied vehicle motor engines in every step. It is possible that the (AI) robotic machine 3D printing skills will be improved more better to compare human 3 D printing workers' skills as well as its 3D printing vehicle motor engine copied product manufacturing speed will also faster than human 3D printing worker's printing copied manufacturing product's speed. Consequently, it will bring positive benefits to any kinds of vehicle engine products productivity number growth to sell different kinds of vehicle engines to vehicle sellers to different country vehicle sale market in order to raise its global vehicle engine sale market competitive effirt and revenue. So, (AI) robotic machine seems really raise productivity growth when it is applied to manufacturing industry.

Why is (AI) learning system the best tool to be applied to manufacturing industry? In fact, future (AI) robotic machine will be one kind of intangible capital to manufacturing organizations to help them to innovate, adjustment costs, organizational changes to be better and new manufacturing skills are needed for successful in every production process.

Historically, most computer programs were created by codifying human knowledge, step-by-step, mapping inputs to outputs by the programmers. In constrast, machine learning systems use categories of general algorithms , e.g. neural networks to figure out the relevant mapping on their own, typically by being fed very large data sets of examples. By using these machine learning methods bring the growth in total data and data processing resources, machines have made impressive gains in perception and cognition, two essential skills for most types of human work.

Nowadays, an increasing number of companies have responded to these high technological opportunities to be applied to manufacturing function aspect, such as Google now describes its focus on " AI first", when Microsoft's CEO says (AI) is the " ultimate breakthrough" in technology. Their optimism about (AI) is not just cheap talk. They are making heavy investments to apply (AI) technology in manufacturing function aspect. The possibility is that the gains of (AI) manufacturing function new technologies are already attainable to different kinds of manufacturing industries. Assuming the (AI) robotic manufacturing worker technologies are at least partially rivalrous. Their effect on averge productivity growth is modest overall, and is virtually not essential need fo median worker. For instance, two of the most profitable uses of (AI) for targeting and pricing online ads. and for automated trading of financial instruments, both applications with many zero-sum aspects.

Hence, I predict that future one day will occur many low skillful level workers lose their manufacturing jobs in factories, due to many manufacturing firms choose to apply (AI) robotic machines to replace human labor workers to help them to manufacture any products in order to achieve increasing productivity growth and reducing manufacturing labor number and wages and raising revenue aims. It is really a good reason to be optimistic about the future productivity growth potential of new technologies, such as (AI) robotic machine to be replaced to the traditional slow speed and low efficient productivity and high cost manufacturing method or technique to any factories.

In conclusion, due to manufacturers expect to raise productivity growth aim. It has two main sources of the delay between recognition of a new technology, such as (AI) robotic machine's potential and its measurable effects. One is that it takes time to build the stock in the new technology to a size sufficient enough to have an aggregate effect. The other is that complementary investments are necessary to obtain the full benefit of the new technology, such as (AI) robotic manufacturing technology and it takes time to discover and develop these complements and to implement them. When, the fundamental importance of the core invention and its potential for society might be clearly recognizable at the outset, the myriad necessary co-invention, obstacles and adjustment needed along the way award discovery over time if future one day had another kind new manufacturing technology which can replace (AI) robotic manufacturing method to be better. Hence, it explains that futuer there are many manufacturing industries choose to apply (AI) robotic machines to replace human workers in factory manufacturing environments in order to achieve the raising of productivity growth in efficient way aim more easily.

4.1 Apply (AI) technology to raise US lighting product productivity growth

Future, (AI) robotic machines can help warehouse workers to apply 3D printers to manufacture any copied different kinds of lighting products to raise productivity growth to satisfy different lighting design consumers needs in efficient way and fast manufacturing speed to manufacture different kinds of design lighting products to satisfy different lighting home and shopping center customers' needs. Every country has itself lighting market customer characterization because different lighting products have different types, functions, colors, designs to attract lighting customer choice. Lighting consumers functions include home reading room, dinner room, bed room, toilet function; office lighting working environment function; shopping center shopping environment functionl transportation tools driving at night etc. different light functions.

What are US lighting product unique characterizations? In US future lighting consumption market. Its lighting products will be focused on their unique advantages to beneficial any lighting consumers. US lighting product manufacturers will need to implement technological research such as: lighting energy saving technology. Energy saving is consumed by light sources in US, lighting technologies how many are installed, where they are installed, the performance attributes are of the installed stock of lighting technologies. So, future US lighting product is needed energy saving technology to help lighting consumers to reduce electricity expenditure at residential, commercial and industrial places for office, home, education, retail, public or private car driving light etc. different light needs. So, effective lighting energy saving technology will help public and business and personnel lighting users to reduce much electricity expenditure. So, lighting energy saving technology will be the most importnt factor to influence future potential light consumers to choose to buy the lighting product manufacturer's any lighting products to compare attractive design, style, shape, color , size light product appearance factors. Because in general, any lighting product consumers will like any lighting products can spend less electricity in order to reduce electricity expenditure when they use every day.

Hence, future US key elements of lighting product sale successful factor, any US lighting product sale market will need have these elements, such as: quantity, type, application, and energy use of stationary lighting in the US. Performance characteristics of lighting technologies, trends, drivers and barriers to improved efficiency in the lighting market. Opportunities for energy savings through advances in lighting technology and adoption of best practices, overview of ongoing lighting research in the public and private sectors. It is not only only for lighting product sale in US domestic sale market. It is also included to lighting products export overseas market. Because global lighting product consumers consider how to consume less electricity to use lighting product in order to save electricity energy and expenditure. So, lighting energy -saving technology is value consideration to any US lighting product manufacturers in the future lighting sale market development.

Who will be US future energy -saving lighting product consumption target? I shall indicate as below: Residential consumption target can include manufactured residential , family manufactured business, lighting product consumer who needs lighting product to in their family factory, so they expect to spend less electricity for lighting expenditure in those family manufacturing proceed. Residential single family and multi-family either less than 4 units or 4 or more units, who needs lighting product when they have need to bath or eat dinner or read ot watch television any indoor activities when they are living in their residential homes at night. So, they also expect to buy energy- saving lighting products to reduce their electricity consumption expenditure. Another lighting product consumers are commercial lighting users. This commercial lighting consumer number will be large and their lighting electricity needs will also be much, due to they use light for commercial functions. Such as vacant, office/professional, laboratory, warehouse/non-refrigerated, food sales, public order/safety, health care (out patient) , warehouse (refrigerated), public assembly, religious worship, education, food service, health care (inpatient), hospital ward room patient light service, surgeon room medical surgeon light function , hotel/motel/dorm room light function, shopping mall/center light function for shopping customers, retail shops, excluding shopping mall lighting function etc. different commercial functions. So, lighting commercial customers number and their light needs will be more, due to commercial clients need to turn on lighting products in their stores or hospitals or warehouses etc. different indoor places to use in all days in possible.

Otherwise, residential family lighting users will only use light at night , due to who need to leave their homes to go to offices to work or go to schools to study. So, they will stay at house at night in common. Even, if they stay at homes in the morning or afternoon. They won't need to use lighting at this sunny time. So, residential light consumers will only use lighting product at night in common. Also, it will influence their demand of lighting products' design, color, energy -saving function. Their demand won't be very high. Otherwise, commercial lighting product consumers, they will often need light to help them to serve their clients or serve themselves in offices, hospitals, warehouses, schools, hotels, shopping malls (centers) etc. different places. So, this often useful functions influence their lighting products' design, type, color, what manufacturing materiall is used and the most important need is energy-saving demand, due to the light consumers can save more money to use lesser electricity. So, their lighting product demands are higher to compare residential lighting product consumers. This issue is US lighting product manufacturers need to consider before they decide how to manufacture any lighting products to sell to US domestic or export to overseas lighting market.

The final light consumer target is industrial consumption users. I believe that they will be the most need of light consumers. Because they will need light working environment to help their workers to work ot manufacture any products in factories. The industrial consumers include food product manufacturers, tobacco product manufacturers, textile mill product manufacturers , appear and other textile product manufacturers, apparel and other textile product manufacturers, lumber and wood product manufacturers, furniture and fixtures product manufacturers, paper and allied product manufacturers, printing and publishing product manfacturers, chemicals and allied product manufacturers, petroleum and coal product manufacturers, rubber and miscellaneous plastics product manufacturers, leather and store, glass product manufactuers , primary metal industries manufacturers, fabricated metal product manufactuers, industrial machinery and equipment product manufacturers , electronic and electric equipment manufacturers, transportation equipment manufacturers. Due to they need many workers to help them to manufacture any products in factories. So, enough light environment is important to influence their productivities and efficiencies. So , they will need to buy many lighting products to assist their workers to work anywhere in factories. So, anywhere in factories will need much light to let workers to feel comfortable and visable . So, this industrial light consumers target will be the lighting product's main consumers because they must need to buy many lighting products to let their workers to work in enough light factory environment, even if any lighting products are damaged or used to long time, they will buy other better quality new lighting products to replace these any one of damaged or old lighting products.

In conclusion, it seems that industrial lighting customer number ought be the highest and their demand to lighting products' light quality , such as reducing the lowest dark environment, energy-saving function, lighting products' safety and lighting products' durable and even reasonable price demand which will be the most top to compare othe kinds of lighting product consumers in US , even overseas export lighting market. All US lighting manufacturers ought need to concern how to design the attractive different kinds of lighting product styles to satisfy whese different kinds of lighting product consumers' needs, instead of design aspect, energy-saving technology, light solor, size, reasonable price etc. different factors will influence lighting consumer number.

Reference

Economic research service, factors affecting US pork consumption, 2004

Economic research service, USDA ,U.S. Department Of Agriculture Economic Research Service (ERS)

Girod, B. and De Haan P 2010 More or letter ? A model for changes in household greenhouse gas emissions due to higher income J. Indust. Ecol. 14 31-49.

Meinshauen M et al 2011. The RCP greenhouse gas concentrations and their extensions from 1765 to 2300 clim._change 109 213-41.

Palley Thomas I. 2002 " Economic contradictions coming home to roost? Does the U.S. economy face a long-term aggregate demand generation problem? Journal of post Keynesian Economics, Fall 2002, vol. 25 no. 19

Setterfield , mark, 2010, " Real wages , aggregate demand and the macroeconomic travails of the U.S. economy. Diagnosis and prognosis. " Trinity college department of economic working paper 10-05.

State of the plate , 2015. study on America's consumption of fruit and vegetables, product for better helth foundation, U.S.

Van Ruijven B. De Vries B. Van Vuuren DP and Van Der Sluijs, JP 2010 . A global model for residential energy use: uncertainty in calibration to regional data energy 35 269-82.